...ned on or before

KT-239-090

112 546

051345

THE HENLEY COLLEGE LIBRARY

Metal Crafting Workshop

Metal Crafting Workshop

Marie Browning

Sterling Publishing Co., Inc.

New York

PROLIFIC IMPRESSIONS PRODUCTION STAFF:

Editor in Chief: Mickey Baskett
Copy Editor: Phyllis Mueller
Graphics: Dianne Miller, Karen Turpin
Styling: Lenos Key
Photography: Jerry Mucklow
Administration: Jim Baskett

Every effort has been made to insure that the information presented is accurate. Since we have no control over physical conditions, individual skills, or chosen tools and products, the publisher disclaims any liability for injuries, losses, untoward results, or any other damages which may result from the use of the information in this book. Thoroughly read the instructions for all products used to complete the projects in this book, paying particular attention to all cautions and warnings shown for that product to ensure their proper and safe use.

No part of this book may be reproduced for commercial purposes in any form without permission by the copyright holder. The written instructions and design patterns in this book are intended for the personal use of the reader and may be reproduced for that purpose only.

Library of Congress Cataloging-in-Publication Data

Browning, Marie.
  Metal crafting workshop / Marie Browning.
       p. cm.
  Includes index.
  ISBN-13: 978-1-4027-2450-3
  ISBN-10: 1-4027-2450-0
1. Metal-work. I. Title.
TT205.B76 2006
745.56--dc22

2006002927

2 4 6 8 10 9 7 5 3 1

Published by Sterling Publishing Co., Inc.
387 Park Avenue South, New York, NY 10016
© 2006 by Prolific Impressions, Inc.
Distributed in Canada by Sterling Publishing
c/o Canadian Manda Group, 165 Dufferin Street,
Toronto, Ontario, Canada M6K 3H6
Distributed in the United Kingdom by GMC Distribution Services,
Castle Place, 166 High Street, Lewes, East Sussex, England BN7 1XU
Distributed in Australia by Capricorn Link (Australia) Pty. Ltd.
P.O. Box 704, Windsor, NSW 2756, Australia

Printed in China
All rights reserved

Sterling ISBN-13: 978-1-4027-2450-3
ISBN-10: 1-4027-2450-0

For information about custom editions, special sales, premium and corporate purchases, please contact Sterling Special Sales Department at 800-805-5489 or specialsales@sterlingpub.com.

ACKNOWLEDGMENTS

I thank these manufacturers for their generous contributions of quality products and support in the creation of the projects.

For metal sheets, metal mesh, metallic paste wax, aluminum armature wire, metal stamp pads, wire lantern forms, embossing tools, and texture plates: AMACO – American Art Clay Co., Inc., www.amaco.com

For adhesives for all crafting surfaces, including Gem-Tac, Dazzel-Tac, and Glass, Metal & More for metal projects: Beacon Adhesives, www.beaconcreates.com

For supplies for tin piercing, including tools, patterns, and metal panels: Country Accents, www.piercedtin.com

For decorative scrapbook paper, bottle caps, 1" round bottle cap stickers, mini clips, and metal embellishments: Design Originals, www.d-originals.com

For metal embellishments, including floral brad charms, charm labels, mini tags, jump rings, and metal gift tags: Nunn Design, www.nunndesign.com

For FolkArt acrylic craft paints, dimensional paints, and varnishes: Plaid Enterprises Inc., www.plaidonline.com

For wooden surfaces and tin tiles: Stone Bridge Collection www.stonebridgecollection.com

For metal embossing tools, texture plates, texture wheels, and heavy-duty double-sided adhesive: Ten Seconds Studio, www.tensecondsstudio.com

About Marie Browning

Marie Browning is a consummate craft designer who has made a career of designing products, writing books and articles, and teaching and demonstrating. You may have been charmed by her creative acumen but not been aware of the woman behind it; she has designed stencils, stamps, transfers, and a variety of other award-winning product lines for art and craft supply companies. As well as writing numerous books on creative living, Marie's articles and designs have appeared in numerous home decor and crafts magazines.

Marie Browning earned a Fine Arts Diploma from Camosun College and attended the University of Victoria. She is a Certified Professional Demonstrator, a design member of the Crafts and Hobby Association (CHA), and a board member of the Society of Craft Designers (SCD). Marie also serves on the committee for SCD that researches and writes about upcoming trends in the arts and crafts industry. In 2004 she was selected by *Craftrends* trade publication as a Top Influential Industry Designer.

She lives, gardens, and crafts on Vancouver Island in Canada. She and her husband Scott have three children: Katelyn, Lena, and Jonathan. Marie can be contacted at www.marie browning.com

Other Books by Marie Browning Published by Sterling

- *Casting for Crafters* (2006)
- *Paper Mosaics in an Afternoon* (2006)
- *Snazzy Jars: Glorious Gift Ideas* (2006)
- *Jazzy Baskets* (2005)
- *Purse Pizzazz* (2005)
- *Really Jazzy Jars* (2005)
- *Totally Cool Polymer Clay for Kids* (2005)
- *Totally Cool Soapmaking for Kids* (2004, reprinted in softcover)
- *Wonderful Wraps* (2003, reprinted in softcover)
- *Jazzy Jars* (2003, reprinted in softcover)
- *Designer Soapmaking* (2003, reprinted in German)
- *300 Recipes for Soap* (2002, reprinted in softcover and in French)
- *Crafting with Vellum and Parchment* (2001, reprinted in softcover with the title *New Paper Crafts*)
- *Melt & Pour Soapmaking (2000, reprinted in softcover)*
- Hand Decorating Paper (2000, reprinted in softcover)
- *Memory Gifts* (2000, reprinted in softcover with the title *Family Photocrafts*)
- *Making Glorious Gifts from Your Garden* (1999, reprinted in softcover)
- *Handcrafted Journals, Albums, Scrapbooks & More* (1999, (reprinted in softcover)
- *Beautiful Handmade Natural Soaps* (1998, reprinted in softcover with the title *Natural Soapmaking*)

Contents

Welcome to My Metal Crafting Workshop

The gleam of metal is irresistible, and working with metal is exciting. Metal is versatile, too. The attractive shiny surfaces of brass, tin, aluminum, and copper can convey informal whimsy and formal elegance and suit a range of decorating styles. Metal can be pierced, punched, cut, colored, embossed, twisted, folded, and hammered. It can be used to create and decorate a wide variety of objects – sophisticated tableware, romantic mirrors and vases, picture frames and boxes, and ornaments for house and garden, to name but a few.

The projects in this book – more than 45 in all – are made with all things metal – metal wire, metal sheets, a variety of metal embellishments, and even found metal. Crafters at all skill levels will find intriguing ideas for making decorative accessories and gifts. Both new and time-honored techniques will charm you as you explore the joy of working with metal. All projects include full color photographs, step-by-step instructions, and complete patterns.

The sections about types of metal used for crafting and the tools and equipment to use tell you what you need to know to get started and where to find supplies. Information about basic metal crafting techniques makes it easy to get started. You'll explore simple techniques for twisting wire and bending metal sheeting to form shapes. You'll learn about embossing metals and new techniques for repousse. You can try your hand at traditional piercing and discover the satisfaction of working with recycled and reclaimed metals. Enjoy this creative journey.

Marie Browning

Metals

Some metals are better than others for crafting, and it helps to know a bit about metals and the types of metal available for crafting before you shop for supplies. Copper, tin, and aluminum are base elements and cannot be created from other materials. Brass and pewter are metal alloys (mixtures of two or more metals). Brass is made from copper and zinc; traditionally, pewter is made from tin and lead. Lead-free pewter, a better choice for toxic-free crafting, is now available.

Metal is labeled and referred to by its gauge, a standard of measurement for thickness (as in metal sheeting) or diameter (as in wire). The higher the gauge, the thinner the metal.

Metal Sheets

SHEET METAL

Metal sheeting is sold as flat pieces and on rolls. Heavier tin and brass sheet metal (30 to 40 gauge) are best for piercing. Thick brass sheeting is found in hardware stores, and tin sheets can be purchased where tin piercing tools are sold. **Flashing**, found in hardware stores, can also be used where a thicker metal sheet is required.

TILES

Square tin tiles, reminiscent of the ones used a hundred years ago to cover ceilings in commercial interiors, can be found in a range of sizes, from 4" to 24". They are easy to paint and come in a wide variety of pressed designs and finishes. Find them at home decor outlets.

METAL FOIL

Metal sheet that is lighter than 30 gauge is usually considered a metal foil. Lighter foils – 84 gauge to 196 gauge – are easy to score, cut with scissors, emboss, and texture. They can be found in art supply stores and craft outlets in tin, aluminum, brass, pewter, and copper and in colors, including matte black, which is used for the Colored Pencil Repousse technique. Foil sheets are packaged in rolls and come in a range of lengths and widths.

RECYCLED METAL

Recycled metal from beverage cans can be used for smaller projects; some preparation is required and because the metal from cans is a bit stiffer, it's harder to emboss, but the results are good and the metal is readily available and virtually free.

Examples of metal sheet, including brass and tin heavy- and medium-weight sheeting, tin tiles, lightweight aluminum foils, lightweight copper sheet, and a recycled beverage can.

Metal Mesh

Wire cloth, commonly used for making window screens and filters, is available in aluminum, brass, bronze, and copper and is sold by the foot or in packages of folded sheets or on rolls at hardware stores, building supply centers, and crafts stores.

Mesh is identified by the number of holes per inch. For example, finer, cloth-like mesh woven with finer gauge wire is 80; number 8 mesh is made with a heavier wire. Larger-size mesh is identified by the size of the mesh opening, from 1/8" to 1/2" sizes.

Fine mesh can be cut easily with scissors; for larger mesh, metal cutters or wire cutters are needed. Mesh is pliable and easy to mold – you can easily transform a flat piece of mesh by molding, crimping, twisting, expanding, or folding it to create three-dimensional shapes.

Examples of metal mesh, including woven copper and brass (size 80), 1/8" aluminum sparkle mesh and copper mesh, 3/8" diamond-shape aluminum mesh, and size 8 square-weave woven brass.

Metal Tape

Metal tape comes in copper, brass, and silver-colored aluminum in 1/8", 1/4" and 1/2" widths. The thin metal foil strips are self-adhesive and come with a protective paper backing. You remove the backing as you apply the tape, then burnish well to adhere. After application, metal tape can be coated with a waterbase clear glossy sealer to prevent tarnishing.

Metal tape can be found where supplies for stained glass crafting are sold and at hardware stores. Store metal tapes in zipper-top plastic bags to keep them from oxidizing.

Making Your Own Metallic Tape:
You can also make metallic tape in custom widths and colors from lightweight metal sheets and double-sided tape. You will need a cutting mat, a craft knife or steel point, and a metal ruler.

Here's how:
1. Using the markings on the cutting mat and the ruler as guides, cut strips from the metal sheets with an art knife or steel point. (The steel point gives a slightly rough edge to the metal strip; a craft knife gives a smoother edge.)
2. Apply double-sided tape to the backs of the strips.

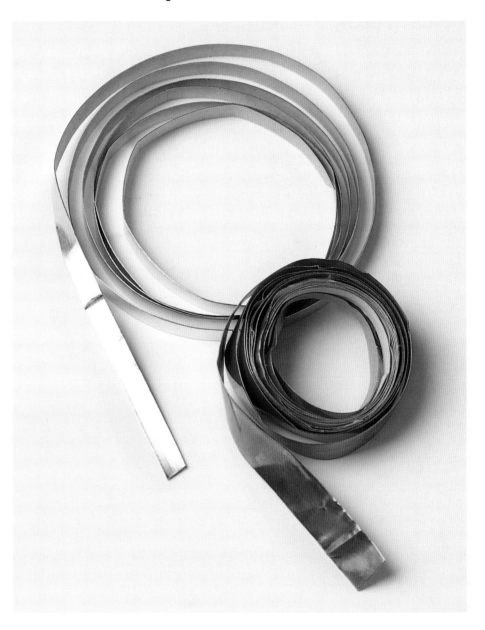

THE HENLEY COLLEGE LIBRARY

13

Metal Wire

Wire – pliable metal strands – comes in a variety of thicknesses and lengths by the foot, in packages, and on spools or paddles. Wire is measured and labeled by its thickness, called the gauge – the higher the gauge, the thinner the wire. Coat hanger wire, for example, is 16 gauge, and thin beading wire is 34 gauge.

COLORED WIRE

Stiffer wires hold their shape after bending better than others but are harder to work with; armature wire is easy to bend but won't hold a shape. Twisting wires together can yield interesting decorative effects as well as make the wire stronger.

Gold-colored wire is usually made of brass or bronze; silver-colored wire may be sterling silver, steel, aluminum, or tin-coated copper. Wire also comes in a variety of colors, which can be incorporated into the metal. Colored wire also may be vinyl-coated. Even wire that is used everyday, such as coat hangers and paper clips, can be twisted and shaped into decorative projects.

ARMATURE WIRE

Non-corroding aluminum armature wire is easy to bend and will not tarnish. Sculptors use it for building frames for papier mache, clay, and wire mesh projects. Armature wire can be found in thick (1/4"), medium (3/16"), and thin (1/16") diameters in art supply and craft stores. Aluminum wire, found in the electrical departments of building supply centers, can be used like armature wire. Aluminum wire is especially nice when flattened with a hammer for a forged appearance. Pounding makes the wire stronger, and it's easier to glue on flat surfaces when flattened.

STEEL WIRE

Steel wire can be found in the garden departments of home improvement stores. It's used to create trellises and wire supports for plants and comes in silver, green, and black, usually in 19 gauge. Steel wire can rust over time and when exposed to weather, but that may be a welcome effect. Because steel wire is stiff, it is excellent for hangers and projects where a strong wire that keeps its shape is needed. Steel wire used for floral design comes on paddles in 24 and 26 gauges. Brown paper-wrapped steel wire, which is intended to look natural in floral designs, is thicker (16-gauge).

COPPER WIRE

Copper wire is found in hardware stores in a variety of gauges, and is pliable and easy to work with. Buss wire, a tin-coated copper wire, is shiny and inexpensive. Find it in hardware and crafts stores. Crafts stores also carry rolls of copper wire colored in a wide variety of hues from 16 gauge (thicker) to 34 gauge (very thin). Colorful vinyl-coated copper wires are available in 16 gauge to 24 gauge.

BULLION

Bullion is a very fine, tightly coiled wire used in seasonal decorations and floral design. It was first used on Christmas ornaments and as tree tinsel in the Victorian era. To use bullion, cut a 6" piece and pull gently to expand to a 30" piece, then form and shape. Do not pull so hard that you stretch out the kinks – it's the kinks that give the wire its sparkle-y look.

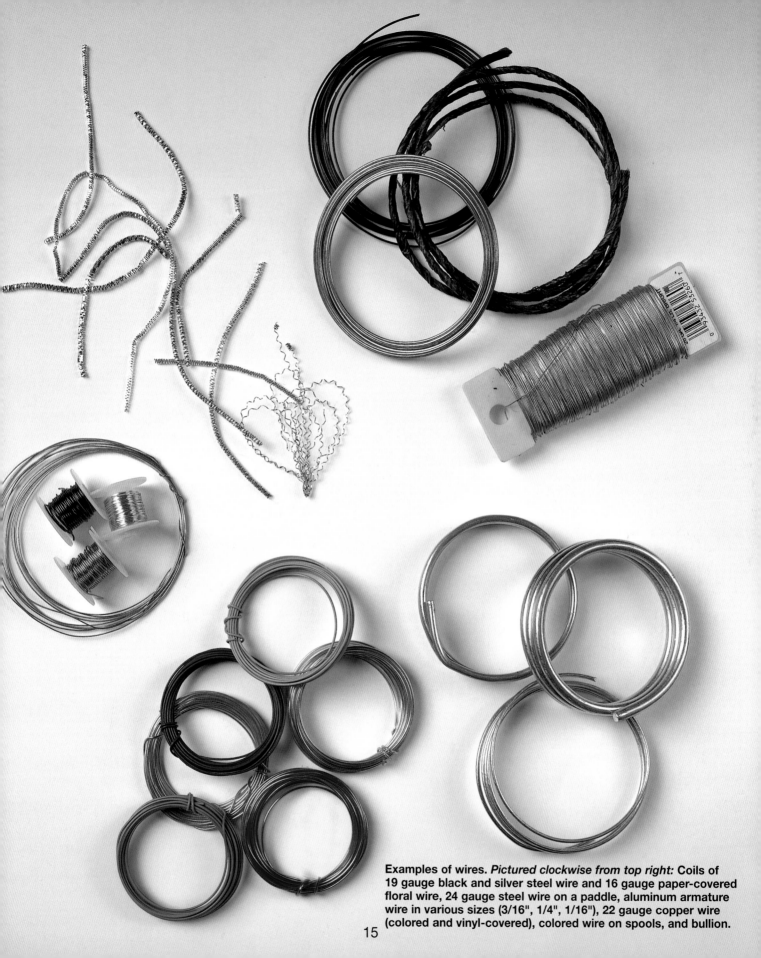

Examples of wires. *Pictured clockwise from top right:* Coils of 19 gauge black and silver steel wire and 16 gauge paper-covered floral wire, 24 gauge steel wire on a paddle, aluminum armature wire in various sizes (3/16", 1/4", 1/16"), 22 gauge copper wire (colored and vinyl-covered), colored wire on spools, and bullion.

15

Metal Embellishments

Metal embellishments include items for attaching pieces together, such as brads, eyelets, and clips, and decorations, such as metal letters, stickers, and charms. Scrapbooking outlets, bead stores, hardware, stationery, and art supply stores are all good places to search for embellishments. They make your projects interesting and give them a finished appearance.

METAL STICKERS

Metal stickers are made of real metals, such as pewter and copper, and of foil-covered plastic. Both types are found in a wide variety of patterns and motifs. Many metal stickers have an adhesive that will adhere the stickers to a metal surface; if the sticker does not hold well, use a metal glue to attach it.

LABEL HOLDERS

Label holders and **hinges** are both decorative and functional. When gluing them to a metal project, place brads into the nail holes to simulate the appearance of nail heads for a finished look.

FOUND METAL EMBELLISHMENTS

Bottle caps can be bought in crafts stores or recycled. They look like little round picture frames when they are flattened with a rubber mallet and decorated with 1" round stickers. **Metal discs** can be recycled from frozen juice cans or purchased in packages. Hardware and antiques stores and yard sales, tag sales, salvage yards, and auctions can be sources for a wide variety of metal embellishments – new and used – including keys, hinges, doorknobs, drawer and cabinet pulls, keyholes, and latches.

BRADS

Brass brads in a variety of sizes can be found in stationery stores; look in the scrapbooking aisles of crafts stores for brads a huge variety of shapes and colors, including some with decorative tops.

CHARMS, LABELS, AND TAGS

These can be found at bead stores or in card making and rubber stamp stores. Small engraved tags are delightful accents, and larger charm labels come with templates so you can customize them with stickers and decorative papers. They are available in silver, brass, and copper colors and can be attached with jump rings or small brads. Also look for laser-cut **metal letters and words** and **metal trims**.

EYELETS

Eyelets range in size from very tiny to large. They come in decorative forms and many colors. When you buy eyelets, you'll also need the tools for installing them. Check the package for recommendations.

Equipment
Basic Tools

METAL CUTTERS

Craft scissors can cut lightweight metal and mesh sheets, but cutting metal will tend to dull the scissors so it's a good idea to dedicate an older pair for this task.

Metal cutters easily cut through metal sheets (up to 30-gauge thickness) without leaving a sharp edge.

A **steel point** can be used to cut medium- and lightweight metal sheets.

HAMMERS

For metal piercing and general metal work, an 8 oz. **ball peen hammer** works best. The head of a ball peen (machinist's) hammer is flat on one end and rounded on the other. A **rubber mallet** is useful for taking out dents and curves from metal sheets. Some metal workers prefer rawhide mallets because they are less likely to mar the metal sheet. When working with wire, many jewelry artists use a **nylon-tipped hammer**, which will not mar surfaces.

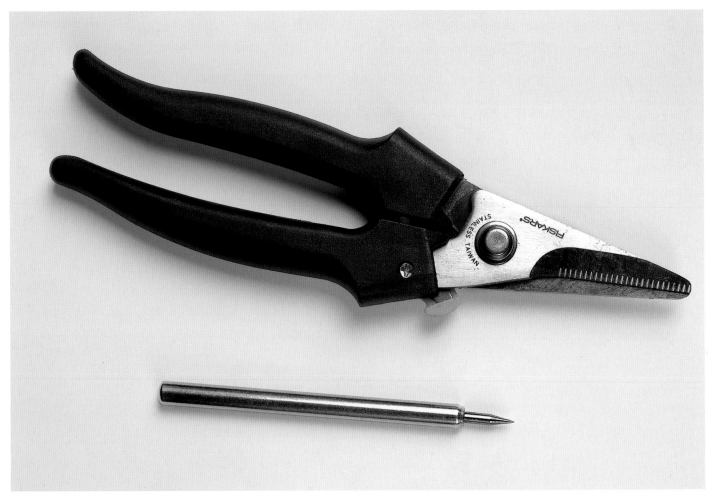

Pictured: metal cutters and steel point.

AWL

An **awl** is the basic tool for making holes in metal. Use it for piercing designs or for making holes for inserting eyelets and brads.

PERMANENT MARKER

Use a fine-tip permanent black marker for marking placements, cuts, and scores on metal surfaces.

WIRE CUTTERS

Basic wire cutters come in a variety of sizes. Thicker wire requires larger, sturdy cutters; thinner wire can be cut with smaller jeweler's wire cutters. Thin beading wire can be cut with scissors. As cutting wire dulls scissors, dedicate an older pair for this purpose.

PLIERS

Pliers are used for bending metal sheets and for bending, coiling, and twisting wires. The type use depends on the task:

Needlenose pliers have fine, textured tips that tightly grasp metals. They are handy for manipulating the wire into shapes.

Flat-nose pliers have a larger grip area and are smooth inside. This is an advantage when you do not want to make a mark on the metal, but the smooth surface makes it more difficult to grasp heavier gauge wires.

Round-nose pliers, used in jewelry making, are for forming loops and coils from wire.

METAL RULERS

Metal rulers are handy for marking lines for scoring and cutting and for folding a long straight edge in a metal sheet. An 18" length with a cork backing is best.

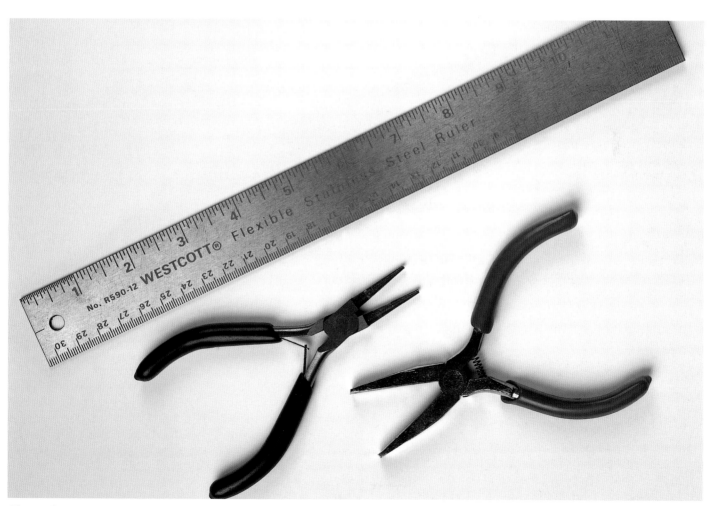

Pictured: metal ruler and pliers

Embossing Tools

Embossing is done from the back of the metal, pushing the metal to shape it. Specialty metal embossing tools are available at most craft or hobby shops and on line. Most embossing projects can be done with a **sharpened wooden stick or dowel**, which is often sold with rolls of medium- or lightweight metal sheet. However, tools made specifically for embossing metal make the work go much faster and yield amazing results.

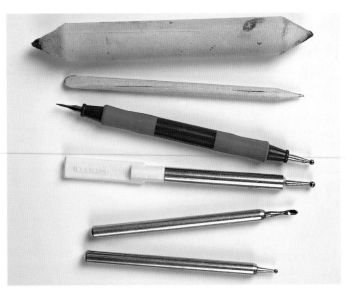

PAPER STUMPS

A **paper stump** is an excellent tool for embossing in large areas. It does not mar the surface of the metal and is my favorite tool for lightly embossing textures. Paper stumps are made from rolled soft paper and are also used in charcoal drawing. They come in a range of sizes with double points, from small (#1) to large (#8). I prefer the #8 size for most embossing jobs. You can renew the point on the stump by sanding with 150-grit sandpaper.

Pictured top to bottom: Tools for embossing – paper stump, a sharpened wooden stick, four tools with pointed, ball, and spoon-shaped tips.

METAL EMBOSSERS

These are shafts like writing instruments with metal ball- or spoon-shaped tips in a variety of sizes from very small to large. Embossing tools with hard plastic (Teflon[r]) tips glide easily on metal surfaces. Find them in a variety of shapes and sizes.

Pictured: Mini roller

EMBOSSING WHEELS

Embossing wheels quickly add texture and decorative borders. **Tracing wheels** also work well for adding lines of texture; they are available in a wide assortment of designs and sizes. Find tracing wheels at fabric stores and decorative wheels at stores that sell tools for metalworking.

ROLLERS AND FOLDERS

Mini rollers are used to flatten folded metals for a sharp, clean edge. They are found at specialty metal tool outlets. You can also use a **bone folder** to press folded metal edges.

EMBOSSING MAT

When embossing metal, you need a firm work surface that gives slightly – if it's too soft, you can easily punch through a lightweight metal sheet and ruin your design; if the surface is too hard, motifs will not be fully embossed. Many metal crafters use a pile of newsprint, thin rubber mat, or a thick piece of suede as an embossing surface. I prefer to use a thin foam sheet, readily available from craft stores. It can be found in the aisle with children's craft supplies.

TEXTURE PLATES

Plastic texture plates are used to create designs and textures on metal sheeting. Thin, clear plates can be used with lightweight metal sheets; thicker, hard plastic plates are for use with medium metal sheets. Find them in crafts and art supply stores.

Tape the metal sheet securely to the surface over the embossing plate with masking tape. Use a paper stump to rub the area and reveal the pattern. With a larger-tip embosser, press the metal around the motifs, then use a smaller embossing tool to outline and refine the embossed design. When finished, lift the embossed metal from the plate.

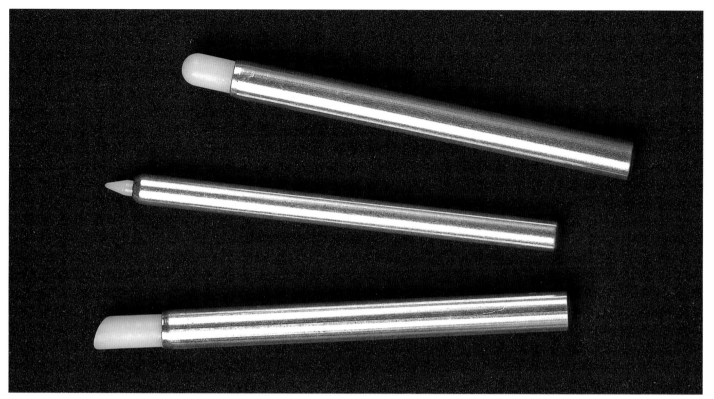

Pictured: Embossing tools with hard plastic tips.

Pictured: Texture plates for embossing.

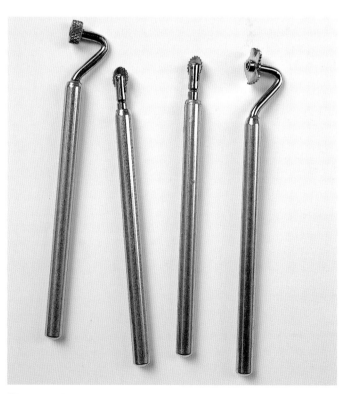

Pictured: Embossing wheels for creating embossed textures.

Piercing Tools

Although a large nail or an awl and a small chisel can be used for most pierced metal projects, specialized piercing tools provide excellent, professional results.

POINT PUNCH

A point punch is the universal hole-making tool. It can make a variety of punctures, from small indentations to 1/8" holes, depending on the force of the hammer blow. A hole made with a point punch leaves a sharp edge on the back of the metal sheet.

HOLE PUNCH

A basic hole punch removes a slug from the metal while making the hole so the back of the metal sheet is smooth, and it makes a uniform-size hole each time. Hole punches come in sizes ranging from 3/32" to 1/8".

METAL CHISEL

A metal chisel makes a smooth elongated hole that is tapered on each end. This basic tool comes in a variety of sizes, from tiny (3/16") to large (5/8").

OTHER PIERCING TOOLS

Other decorative piercing tools make a variety of shaped holes – C-shaped curves, crosses, triangles, ovals (the tool is called a willow punch), squares, diamonds, or leaf shapes.

WORK SURFACE FOR PIERCING

Plywood can be used as a surface for punching metal, but I prefer particle board. A 12" x 16" piece is a good size.

Pictured: Piercing tools and examples of the holes they make; ball peen hammer.

Sanding & Polishing Tools

SANDPAPER & PADS

Fine sandpaper (300 grit or finer) is used to smooth cut edges on metal. I prefer **fine sanding sponges** – I think they are easier to use. Wear gloves to protect your hands and avoid cuts.

Abrasive pads – fine and ultra-fine ones – can be used to dull the surface of metal. They can also be used to remove color from an embossed piece of colored metal.

BRUSHES

A **brass wire brush** is used to create brushed finishes. Work the brush in a small circular motion to softly etch the surface.

STEEL WOOL

Steel wool is less abrasive than sandpaper and can remove spots and rust from metal.

SMOOTHING TOOL

A **plastic smoothing tool** is used to smooth and remove kinks and dents from medium- and lightweight metal and mesh sheets that have gotten bent in storage or from rough handling or to flatten metal sheets that come on rolls. Use the tool on a smooth, hard surface, burnishing (rubbing) the metal sheet with the edge of the tool to remove marks. You can also use the edge of a plastic texture plate (as long as it's free of any marks) for smoothing. The smoothing tool can also add interesting texture to a sheet of lightweight metal. To create the texture, crumple the metal, then smooth it flat.

Adhesives

GLUES

Jewelry glue is a clear-drying, white glue made especially for gluing metals together and gluing metals to other surfaces. Because it takes time to dry completely, it offers the opportunity to readjust placement of items. Clean away excess glue with a damp paper towel after the glue is dry.

Metal glue is good for gluing metal to metal and offers a quick grip. This clear, silicone-based glue gives strong, permanent results. Because this glue can be thick and messy, it's best to use a toothpick to place small amounts. You may need to hold the metal pieces together with weights or clamps while drying. Clean off excess glue by scraping it off the metal with a craft knife after the glue is dry.

Epoxy glue offers the strongest bond. The glue comes in two containers, resin and hardener. Use a wooden craft stick to mix equal amounts of each. I prefer 30-minute epoxy to five-minute epoxy – it provides a superior bond.

TAPE

I like to attach metal sheeting to surfaces with **double-sided tape**, which is available in widths from 1/8" to 1/2" or in large sheets. Choose the strongest tape adhesive you can find. I like the one that's sold for adhering tiny marbles and metal foils. Available at crafts stores, it provides instant adhesion that is strong and permanent.

Burnish the metal well for a strong bond.

Safety

- **Protect your fingers.** The cut ends of wire and edges of metal sheets are very sharp. Wear protective cotton or leather gloves (such as garden gloves) when working with metal to avoid cuts.

- **Protect your eyes.** When cutting wire, always point the wire toward the floor or hold both ends to prevent the wire from flying into your face. Wear eye goggles when cutting wire and snipping ends off metal sheets. Goggles should also be worn when piercing metal.

- **Protect your lungs.** Wear a dust mask when sanding metals.

- **Smooth metal after cutting.** Rub the cut edges of metal with 300 grit sandpaper to remove any barbs and to smooth rough edges.

- **Don't ingest!** Working with metals can leave residues on your hands that you don't want inside your body. To be safe, wash your hands frequently, don't touch your mouth or your eyes, and don't eat or smoke while working with metals.

Basic Techniques
Folding Metal

A **metal ruler** provides a straight, firm edge for folding and prevents the **metal sheet** from crinkling and creasing instead of folding along the scored line.

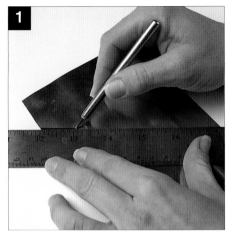

Score: Use a ruler and medium ball embossing tool to score the fold line.

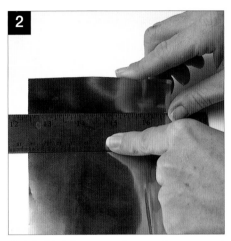

Fold: Holding a ruler to the scored line, firmly fold up the edge.

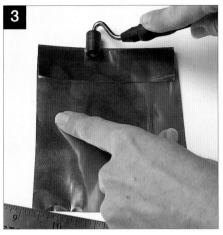

Press: Fold the metal over and press down. Press with a mini roller to make a sharp, crease-free fold.

Cutting Metal

- Use **scissors or metal cutters** to trim or cut shapes from metal sheets and mesh. Which you use depends on the thickness. For 30 to 40 gauge metals, you'll need metal cutters; for thinner metal foils (84 gauge and thinner), use an old pair of scissors.

- Use a **steel point** to make inside cuts in metal and to cut along a straight edge. Working on a soft surface, such as an embossing mat, score the cut with the steel point. Repeat the score, pressing firmly, until the metal breaks. The edge will be slightly rough – sand it smooth with fine sandpaper.

- Use **wire cutters** for cutting wire. Always hold both parts of the wire when cutting to prevent cut ends from flying, and always wear safety goggles.

- **Always smooth the cut edges.** When metal has been cut, the edges can be very sharp. Remove any tiny barbs by trimming with **scissors**. Smooth cut edges by rubbing with fine (300 grit) **sandpaper** or an **abrasive pad**. File any rough spots on the ends with a fine **metal file** or sandpaper.

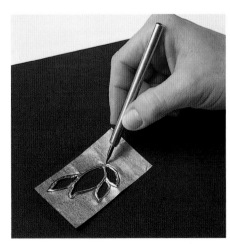

Pictured: Cutting with a steel point.

Hammering

Pounding metal sheets with the ball end of a ball peen hammer quickly gives light- and medium-weight metal sheets an interesting texture. Hammer the metal on a firm but slightly flexible surface, such as a piece of plywood.

Hammering gives wire a forged look and makes the wire stronger and easier to glue to a surface. I prefer to hammer wire on an anvil or smooth hard surface. If you pound the wire flat on a concrete floor or other textured surface, the metal will pick up the texture of the floor. To ensure a smooth surface on hammered wire, hammer on a piece of scrap 30-gauge tin sheet if you don't have an anvil. After a bit of use, the tin sheet will become marred and will need to be replaced.

You can add texture as you flatten wire by pounding with the ball end of a ball peen hammer or by placing a piece of metal mesh over the wire while you hammer.

WIRE CALLIGRAPHY

When you form lettering from wire and pound it flat, you can achieve a thick-to-thin variation in the letters that imitates thick-and-thin calligraphy.

Here's how: After forming the word with wire, hammer selected areas and taper the pounding. TIP: Don't hammer crossed wires (such as the bottom loop in the letter "g") too much – you could cause the wire to break.

FLATTENING BOTTLE CAPS

To flatten a bottle cap, place the cap right side up on a firm surface, such as a piece of plywood, and hammer with a rubber mallet. The cap will flatten nicely, creating a decorative edge around the center. You can use either side. NOTE: This works only with new, unused bottle caps, which can be found in crafts stores in a variety of colors.

Hammered metal with a ball peen hammer.

Pictured: Top row – Front and back of hammered brass metal sheet.

Middle row – Lettering formed with armature wire and hammered at certain points to create different widths.

Bottom row, left to right – Hammered on a smooth surface (anvil), Hammered on a textured surface – concrete floor, Hammered with the round end of a ball peen hammer to give a forged look, Hammered with a piece of metal mesh between to create a texture.

Sanding

Metal can be sanded for safety reasons (smoothing a freshly cut piece) or aesthetic reasons (creating a dull surface). Sanding metal sheeting gives the surface more "tooth" so it will accept paint or decoupage medium better.

DULLING

To dull the surface of metal, rub with a **fine abrasive pad** in a small circular motion. On embossed pieces, dulling the metal provides a pleasing contrast to the shiny, non-embossed areas so the embossing shows up better. You can also use **steel wool** for dulling metal surfaces, but it can leave an oily residue – problematic if you're planning to paint. A **brass wire brush** can add a dramatic finish to metal – use the brush to make small circular scrubbing strokes on the surface.

DISTRESSING

Sanding can also be part of a painted finish. For a distressed look, paint the metal and, when completely dry, sand off some of the paint to reveal some of the metal.

You can also create an interesting texture by sanding away the color on colored metal sheeting.

Here's how:
1. Tape a piece of lightweight colored metal sheet on an embossing plate.
2. Rub with a large embosser or paper stump to create the embossed design.
3. Keeping the metal sheet in place, sand lightly with a fine abrasive pad. The finer the pad, the more control you have on the amount of color you will remove. When the desired effect is achieved, remove the metal sheet from the embossing plate.

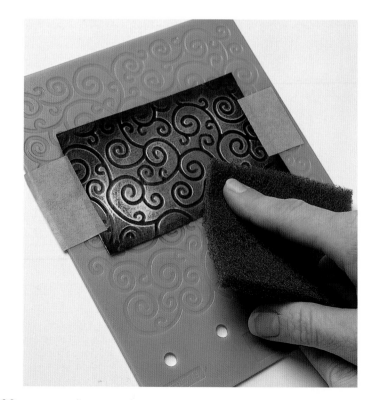

Working with Wire

TWISTING WIRE

Twisting makes a stronger piece of wire and makes wire more decorative. For my easy technique, you need wire, a vise or a clamp, and a pencil or wooden dowel. Use this method to twist short or very long lengths. The twists will be symmetrical and will not unravel, even when cut into shorter lengths. Use a variety of wire colors and gauges for interesting twisted designs.

Here's how:
1. Cut two, three, or four equal lengths of wire.
2. Twist one end of the wire bundle together firmly. Place this end securely in a vise, or clamp it to a sturdy base, such as a countertop.
3. Keeping the wires together and taunt, twist the other ends around a pencil or a wooden dowel.
4. Holding the wires where they meet the pencil, keeping them taunt, twirl the pencil to twist the wire.

BENDING WIRE

With a pair of good needlenose pliers and a simple pattern, it's very easy to bend and shape wire. You simply bend the wire to match the pattern, keeping the wire as smooth and as kink-free as possible. CAUTION: Wear safety goggles to protect your eyes.

When making more than one wire project using the same pattern, a jig can be very helpful. A jig also is useful when working with stiffer (harder to bend) wire. Commercially available plastic jigs with removable pegs are very easy and handy to use. You can also make a jig with plywood and headless nails.

Here's how:
1. Trace the pattern on a piece of plywood.
2. Using a hammer, pound small headless nails on the pattern lines at 1/2" intervals. To use, bend the wire around the nails to form the pattern.

COILING WIRE

It's easiest to coil wire by using a commercially available wire coiler.

WRAPPING WIRE

Wire wrapping techniques are used for wrapping wire around metal objects such as cutlery or the stem of a wine glass. Wrapping a thinner wire (24 gauge to 28 gauge) around a thicker wire is an interesting decorative effect.

To make a **single color wrap**, hold the thinner wire at an 90 degree angle to the thicker wire and wrap the thinner wire around the thicker one, keeping the coils tight and close together. For a **multi-color wrap**, wrap all the wires (the photo shows three colored strands) at the same time, holding them at a 90-degree angle to the thicker wire.

The **candy cane wrap** leaves a bit of the base wire exposed. Hold a single strand or several strands of thinner wires at a 45-degree angle to a thicker wire and wrap at an angle, leaving space as you wrap.

To finish the ends of all the wraps, trim off the excess wire close to the thicker wire and pinch the ends tightly with flat-nose pliers.

THE HENLEY COLLEGE LIBRARY

Working with Metal Mesh

Metal mesh can be folded and shaped much like metal sheets, but the edges can ravel. For that reason, it's a good idea to cut the mesh piece a little larger than the size needed in case the edges ravel. Folding the edges prevents the mesh from unraveling and makes the edges smooth.

Finer metal mesh cloth can be sewn like fabric and used to create pouches and purses. The larger mesh can be stretched and expanded to create three-dimensional shapes.

Attaching Metal

There are many ways to hold metal pieces together. The easiest is to use a system of eyelets, brads, or wiring to join the pieces securely.

Many glues can be used to attach metal to wood and metal to metal. Follow the manufacturer's instructions for use, work in a well-ventilated area to protect yourself from fumes, and don't let the glue come into contact with your skin.

Embossing Metal

Repousse is an ancient technique for shaping and ornamenting malleable metal by hammering from the back side. The most famous contemporary sculpture created with repousse is the Statue of Liberty in New York City – copper sheets were hammered over wooden structures to shape each piece. License plates are a form of modern repousse that we see every day.

Repousse means "pushed up" in French; when the metal is pushed with tools from the back to create subtle designs, it's called metal embossing. Creating designs by pressing on the right side of the metal is called chasing (it's the opposite of embossing). The two techniques, used together, create a finished embossed metal piece. Softer metals such as copper and tin are usually attached to a permanent base, such as wood, stone or other metals, to retain the shape after embossing.

For deep embossing on lightweight metal sheets, it's a good idea to fill in the back of the design to prevent the embossed areas from collapsing. You can buy a filler paste or use hot glue or dimensional paint to add support. Filling the back for support is recommended for a project such as a book cover or a purse, which will be handled and moved around.

EMBOSSING TECHNIQUE

1. **Transfer the pattern.** Trace the pattern on tracing paper, using a fine-tip permanent black marker. Tape the pattern on a medium- or lightweight metal sheet with masking tape and place on a hard surface. Use a small-tip embossing tool to trace over the pattern lines. (This will transfer the pattern to the metal without embossing it – you should be able to see the pattern on the back of the metal sheet.) Remove the paper pattern and place the metal sheet on an embossing mat, right side down. Using the small-tip embossing tool, trace the pattern lines on the back side of the metal, making an embossed outline of the design. **See photo 1.**

2. **Emboss the design.** With the metal sheet still on the embossing mat, right side down, emboss the design. Choose an embossing tool (a large spoon-shaped embosser or a paper stump) to fit the size of the motif. Press gently to slowly and evenly stretch the metal. **See photo 2.**

3. **Chase (refine) the embossing.** Place the metal sheet on the embossing mat, right side up. With a small ball-tip embosser or a tool with a hard plastic tip, press around all the motifs to sharpen the design and make the details stand out. **See photo 3.**

4. **Add details and textures.** With the metal sheet on the embossing mat, add details to both the front and back. **See photo 4.**

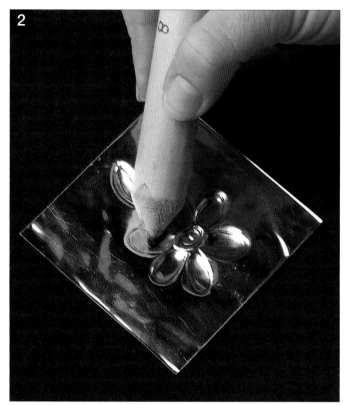

Dimensional Repousse

I developed this technique as an easy way to provide an embossed design in the metal sheet that will not collapse after the embossing is finished. This uncomplicated embossing method enables you to use a variety of patterns and designs, and the supplies are easy to obtain.

NOTE: Be sure the dimensional paint and sticky glue have cured and dried thoroughly before adding the metal sheet and embossing the design.

You will need:
- **Dimensional paint**, which is readily available in craft stores. It can be found in both the fabric painting and the paper crafts departments. It comes in a bottle with an applicator tip that squeezes out the paint in a thin line.
- **Sticky glue** – This glue stays sticky even after it dries. Find it with metal leafing and foiling supplies. *Option:* Use a spray adhesive that stays sticky after it has cured.
- **Base** – A wood, metal, or plastic surface or a piece of thick card stock that can be glued on your project.
- **Embossing tools** – Paper stump, fine and medium ball-tip embossers
- **Metal sheets** – Medium to light-weight gauge
- **Tracing paper** and fine-tip black marker, for tracing designs
- **Transfer paper**, for transferring the design to the base
- *Optional:* Glass paints or embossing wheels, for decorating

Here's how:
1. Trace the pattern on tracing paper, using a permanent black marker. Use transfer paper to transfer the pattern to the base surface. **See photo 1.**
2. Go over the pattern lines with dimensional paint. Hold the paint bottle upside down with the nozzle on the surface for an even, bubble-free flow. Let the paint cure for a full 48 hours before proceeding. **See photo 2.**
3. Brush or lightly spray the surface with the sticky glue. Let glue dry until clear – it will still be tacky.
4. Place the metal sheet over the glue and press lightly to adhere it to the surface. Use a paper stump to lightly rub the metal to press it over the dimensional paint to reveal the design. **See photo 3.** With the small embosser, trace around the design, pushing the metal snugly against the painted design lines.
5. Add textures with embossing wheels or glass paint to color the design. **See photo 4.**

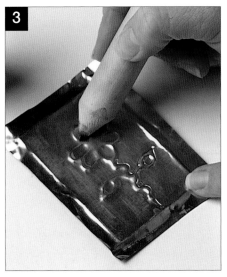

Colored Pencil Repousse

This technique is done on lightweight matte black metal sheets with colored pencils – you color and emboss the front of the metal at the same time. Use it to create embossed panels. When accented with metallic pastes, the technique can be used to make exceptional labels and tags. I found watercolor pencils work best; the softer the pencil, the better the results. You will notice the colors look different on the dark surface, and lighter colors have a more dramatic impact than the darker hues.

You will need:
- Lightweight black matte metal sheet
- Watercolor pencils
- Embossing mat
- Clear matte spray varnish
- Tracing paper and fine-tip permanent black marker

Here's how:
1. **Transfer the pattern.** Trace the pattern on tracing paper, using a permanent black marker. Tape the pattern on the matte black metal sheet with masking tape and place on a hard surface. With a small embossing tool, on the front of the metal sheet, trace over the pattern lines firmly, using the small embossing tool. **See photo 1.** Remove the pattern.

2. **Emboss** Place the metal sheet on the embossing pad, right side up. Use the colored pencils to color the design, working from the center out to the edges.

Leave spaces between the shapes to create the black outlines. Don't color details that you wish to remain black, such as the veins in the flower petals. **See photos 2 and 3.**

3. **Varnish.** To fix the color and give the piece a nice finish, spray with a light coat of clear matte varnish.

Metal Piercing

Pierced tin is an old craft that served practical purposes in times past – the holes in tin lanterns allowed light to shine through and protected the candle from drafts. Pie safes had pierced tin panels that let air circulate around food but kept insects out. Pierced tin, no longer a household necessity, adds a charming decorative element to rooms.

Piercing can be done on 30-gauge (or thinner) metal sheeting. TIP: Practice on a sample piece of metal sheet before starting your project.

Many purchased metal items, such as trays, plates, buckets, and lanterns, can be pierced successfully.

Piercing makes one side of the metal rough and sharp. For my projects, I prefer to use the smooth side as the right side. To me, it looks better, and the sharp edges are not exposed.

Prepare:
1. Cut the metal sheet to size.
2. Wrap the sheet firmly with brown kraft paper. Secure the paper on the back with masking tape. This protects the metal from finger marks and provides a surface for securing the pattern.
3. Trace the pattern on tracing paper. Tape the traced pattern in place on the paper-covered metal sheet. (A pattern can be used about three times before it gets distorted from piercing.)
4. Place the metal sheet, with the pattern attached, on a piece of particle board.

Pierce:
CAUTION: Wear safety goggles to protect your eyes when piercing.
1. Position the piercing tool on one of the dots in the pattern. Tap the tool lightly with the hammer to "set" the punch, then tap again with the hammer – harder this time – to pierce the metal.
2. Repeat the process until you have pierced all the holes in the pattern.

Piercing Pointers:
- The distance between the pierced holes can vary; spacing is a personal preference.
- Work methodically from one hole to the next. If you don't, it's very easy to miss holes in the pattern.
- When you have finished piercing, lift one side of the pattern and check to make sure you did not miss any holes in the design. Pierce any holes you missed, then remove the pattern completely. Adjust the size of the holes, if needed.

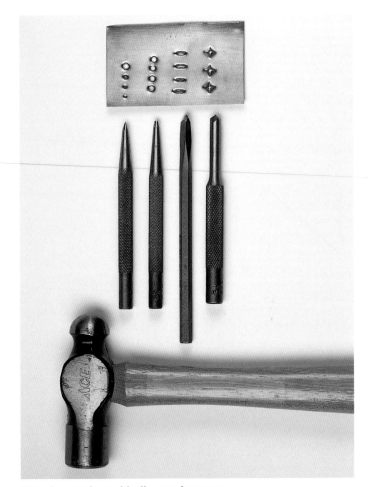

Piercing tools and ball peen hammer

- When using a point punch or a large nail, strike harder for a large hole or more softly for a smaller hole. Practice on a piece of metal so you are familiar with the force needed for holes of different sizes. Variation in hole sizes adds interest in the design.
- For slit-type holes, use a chisel punch tool.
- If the finished piece has bowed a bit during piercing, use a rawhide or rubber mallet to pound the back gently to flatten to the original shape.
- To pierce a pattern into a bucket, a tin can, or a lantern without crushing or bending the item, fill the item with water and place it in the freezer overnight. (The ice will keep the item from collapsing.) Punch the ice-filled item on an old towel to keep it steady. Don't pierce too close to the rim – the ice could shatter.
- Create a matte-finish "background" that highlights the pierced pattern by rubbing with a fine abrasive pad.

EXAMPLES OF PIERCED METAL

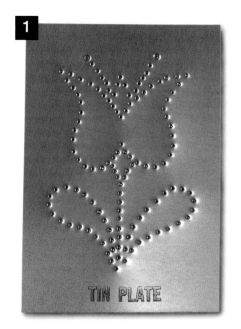

1. TIN PLATE

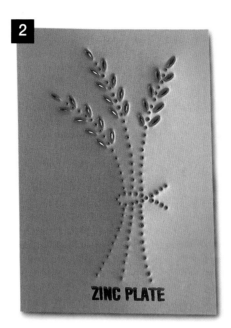

2. ZINC PLATE

3. RUSTED TIN

4. Antiqued Tin

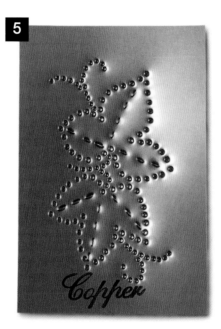

5. Copper

The pierced samples show a variety of designs on different metal sheets.
The samples are courtesy of James Palota, resident artist at Country Accents.

Cleaning Metal

Metal projects can be cleaned by wiping with a soft, dry cloth. If needed, wash the piece in water with some mild, non-abrasive detergent, then wipe dry immediately.

Waxes and polishes are not necessary, but a clear spray varnish can be added to protect metal surfaces from oxidation and color changes. As the spray varnish could alter the finish of the metal, always spray first on a concealed spot to check the appearance of the varnish.

Steel wool or a fine abrasive pad can be used to remove rust and old paint from found metal objects. You can return old metal to its original brilliance quite easily, or leave on some of the rust and/or old paint for an aged, distressed look.

Coloring Metal

HEAT COLORING

By using a heat gun – the kind used for rubber stamp embossing – you can change the color of copper sheeting or copper mesh from its original color to a dull brick red, purple, or blue-white. Altering the color looks especially nice on embossed pieces of copper sheet. Over time, the colors sometimes change but remain a nice contrast to the original copper color.

Here's how:
1. Place the metal on a baking sheet or silicone pad.
2. Hold the embossing gun close to the metal surface. Heat until you see the color change.
3. Allow to cool completely before handling.

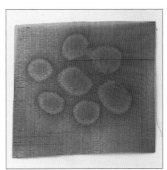

PAINTING METAL

The best paints to use on metal are **specially formulated metal paints**. Available in a wide variety of designer colors, acrylic paints for metal are permanent when fully cured, clean up with soap and water, and are easy to use.

Here's how:
1. Clean the metal surface with rubbing alcohol and let dry to prepare the surface.
2. Use a basecoating brush to apply a thin, even coat of paint. Let dry completely. You may need up to three coats of paint for complete coverage. Let each coat dry thoroughly before adding another.

Other metal paints may require a primer coat. Read the paint manufacturer's instructions carefully for successful results.

Glass paints – paints created for painting on glass – also work on shiny, slick metal surfaces.

Transparent glass paints look particularly nice on metal – the metal color shows through the paint and adds to the effect. Glass paints work well on embossed projects; for dramatic results, you can fill embossed areas of repousse with glass paint.

METALLIC WAXES

Metallic wax pastes come in a wide range of colors, including all the metal colors. They are a wonderful way to add highlights or the look of oxidation to embossed or textured metal projects.

Painted Patina Recipes

Here are my recipes for creating the natural look of weather and age on metal surfaces.

DISTRESSED

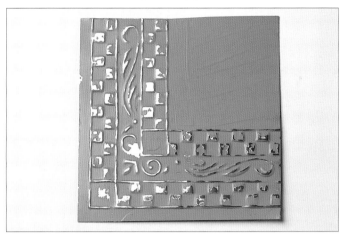

To age the metal, wipe the metal with rubbing alcohol and let dry. Basecoat with two to three coats of metal paint. When completely dry and cured, sand the surface lightly, first with 300-grit sandpaper, then with a fine abrasive pad to refine the look and remove any scratches. (Sand a little or a lot, depending on the look you wish to achieve.)

WASHED

This creates a look that is faded and dulled over time. Wipe the metal with rubbing alcohol and let dry. Apply a thin coat of metal paint, then wipe off the excess immediately with a soft cloth or paper towel. (If you removed too much of the color, repeat and wipe until you achieve the look you want.) When dry, the finish can be refined further by rubbing lightly with a fine abrasive pad. This finish adds subtle color that highlights embossed designs.

RUSTED TIN OR IRON

Rub the metal with rubbing alcohol and let dry. Apply a coat of burnt sienna metal paint with a painting sponge. (The sponge will give a slightly bubbled texture to the paint.) Sponge on some dark patches of dark brown metal paint; if you like, add the dark brown paint while the burnt sienna paint is still wet and blend. Let dry completely and cure. For an authentic-looking finishing touch, apply some turquoise metallic wax paste in some areas to accent the embossed areas and the texture of the paint.

BURNISHED/OXIDIZED

Creates a lustrous metal look. Apply metallic wax paste to the metal (it's easiest to apply with your finger, but you can also use a soft cloth.) When the paste is dry, buff with a soft cloth to burnish to a beautiful metallic luster. For pieces that will be handled frequently, such as jewelry, seal the wax finish with clear, waterbase matte varnish.

Stamping

Any rubber stamp can be used with special inkpads intended for metal or other slick surfaces to add another design element to your work.

Here's how:
1. Wipe the surface with rubbing alcohol and let dry.
2. Ink the stamp as you would for paper. Press stamp on the metal surface with no rocking.
3. Heat set with a craft heat gun to make the design permanent. TIP: Mistakes can be easily removed by wiping with a soft cloth before heat setting.

EMBOSSING STAMPED DESIGNS

Enhancing a Stamped Design

You can stamp an image on metal and use embossing to enhance the stamped image.
1. Wipe the metal with rubbing alcohol and let dry.
2. Stamp the design on the front of the metal sheet and heat set.
3. Place the stamped image right side up on an embossing mat. Use a fine-tip embossing tool to trace the lines of the design.
4. Place the metal, back side up, on the embossing mat. Use embossing tools to emboss the design.
5. Turn over the metal so it's right side up on the embossing mat. Use a fine embossing tool to refine and outline the embossed design.

Embossing, Continued

6. Add color with metallic wax paste or pick up the colored ink from the stamp pad with a cotton swab and wipe on the embossed areas, then heat set the ink.
7. To support the embossed design, fill the back with embossing filler paste, dimensional paint, or hot glue.

Stamp as a Pattern:

You can also use a rubber stamp as a pattern for an embossed design by stamping the design on the back of a metal sheet, but if you stamp on the back the stamping ink won't be visible. TIP: As the image will be reversed, don't use a design with letters or numbers.

1. Wipe the metal with rubbing alcohol and let dry.
2. Stamp the design on the back of the metal sheet and heat set.
3. Place the metal on an embossing mat, back side up, and use a fine embossing tool to trace around the design.
4. Still on the mat with the back side up, use a large-tip embossing tool to emboss the design.

5. Turn the metal right side up and place over the embossing mat. Use a fine embossing tool to refine and outline the design.
6. Add color with metallic wax paste or pick up colored ink from a stamp pad with a cotton swab and wipe on the embossed areas, then heat set the ink.
7. To support the embossed design, fill the back with filler paste, hot glue, or dimensional paint.

Decoupage

I use decoupage medium to adhere paper to metal.

Here's how:

1. Rub the metal with a fine abrasive pad to create "tooth" for better adhesion. Wipe away the dust with a soft cloth, then wipe with rubbing alcohol and let dry.
2. Apply cut paper pieces or paper cutouts, using the decoupage medium as a glue. Let dry.
3. Protect the surface by applying two to three coats of clear varnish (matte, satin, or gloss).

Projects

In this section you'll find instructions for making more than 45 fabulous metal projects. Each project includes a photo, a list of the supplies and tools you'll need, and step-by-step instructions, plus patterns and a wealth of helpful tips. Before you start, be sure to read the sections on Metal, Equipment, and Basic Techniques.

Wire Embellished Vase

Simple wire swirls and beads make spectacular accents for colored glass bottles. If you wish to hang the vase, make the loop from buss wire rather than aluminum wire (buss wire is stiffer; aluminum wire won't hold the weight of the vase). You could substitute coat hanger wire for the buss wire, but coat hanger wire is much harder to bend into swirls.

Supplies

- Green glass bottle, 9" tall
- Medium (3/16") aluminum armature wire
- Buss wire
- 8 to 10 assorted purple glass beads
- Flat-nose pliers
- Wire cutters
- Sandpaper

Instructions

1. Cut a 20" piece of armature wire. Wrap around the neck of the bottle. Bend and swirl both ends of the wire to create a design. (You can use the project photo as a guide or create your own design.) Trim off the excess wire with wire cutters. Sand the ends smooth, if needed.

2. Cut a 20" piece of buss wire. Wrap around the neck of the bottle, making a 1/2" loop at the neck if you wish to hang the vase. Wrap and bend the wire around the thicker wire swirls to add to the design.

3. To make the beaded accents, cut a 6" piece of buss wire and make a 1/2" swirl at one end. Thread on a variety of beads and make a loop at one end. Slip the loop onto the swirled wires. ❏

Fun & Funky Paper Clips

This very simple project is a good introduction to working with wire. Use a small gauge aluminum wire, buss wire, or even large paper clips. Use them every day in your office or to accent a handmade card or scrapbook page. Flattening the wire helps the clip grasp the paper better. To present them as a gift, use a tin container with a glass top. TIP: If you are making a large number of clips for gifts (perfect for co-workers), make a jig or use a commercial jig.

Supplies

- Small gauge aluminum wire, buss wire, or large paper clips, 4" to 6" per shape

- Needlenose pliers

- Wire cutters

- Hammer

- Anvil or other hard surface

Optional: Tin container with glass top, metal label or sticker, jig

Instructions

1. Bend the wire into the shapes, using the patterns as guides, or experiment with other shapes such as hearts or triangles. *Option:* Use a jig.
2. Hammer to flatten evenly on an anvil or other hard surface.
3. *Option:* Place in a tin container. Decorate the clip container with metal, a label, or embossed metal sticker. ❑

PATTERNS

Wire Easels

Handmade wire easels are handy for displaying frames, plates, and other flat objects. The pattern is simple; vary the design for a custom look by bending the wire ends in the front in a heart, a square, or other simple shape rather than the swirl design. You can use thinner wire to make smaller easels.

Supplies

- 1/4" aluminum armature wire, 36"
- Flat-nose pliers
- Wire cutters

Instructions

1. Bend the length of wire in half. Form a 1" loop in the center.
2. Twist the wire together for 3" to 4" inches from the loop.
3. Make a spiral at each end of the wire, using the pliers.
4. Fold up both the wire spirals to make a place for the object to rest. Bend the wire at the base of the twist to form the easel support.
5. Manipulate the wire so it accommodates your frame or plate securely. ❏

Photo Holder

This whimsical photo holder has a doorknob as its base. You could use an old knob for an antique feel or newly purchased knob to create a clean, modern look. When choosing your doorknob, make sure it will sit on a flat surface without wobbling.

Supplies

- Metal doorknob (Clean an old doorknob with steel wool to remove any rust.)
- Lightweight copper metal sheet
- Copper tape, 1/8" wide
- 19-gauge black wire
- Ink pad for metal stamping – Dark brown
- Rubber stamp – Swirled floral design
- 6 mini copper tags with etched words
- Copper jump rings
- 8 to 10 copper E beads
- Metal craft glue
- Wire cutters
- Metal cutters
- Needlenose pliers
- Heat gun

Instructions

1. Measure and cut the copper metal sheet to fit around the neck of the doorknob with a 1/2" overlap.
2. Stamp the copper sheet, using the swirled floral design stamp and dark brown ink. Heat set the ink.
3. Roll the stamped copper piece to create a shaft and glue in place. Apply copper tape to the top and bottom edges. *Option:* Add additional strips of copper tape as accents.
4. Cut eight 10" pieces of black wire. End each piece of wire with a tiny loop, then bend the ends of four pieces into 1" hearts. Bend the ends of the other four pieces to make swirls. To hold the photos, take a piece of wire with a swirl design and a piece with a heart design and twist the wires together about 4" from the decorative ends. (The photo is inserted in the swirl and further secured from the front with a heart piece.)
5. Cut four 8" pieces of wire. Curl and swirl the ends. (You can use as many wire pieces as can fit into the copper shaft – you need two pieces of wire for each photo and one for each charm.)
6. Bundle the ends of the wire pieces together and wrap with a 10" length of black wire. Using the metal glue, securely glue the wire ends into the top of the copper shaft.
7. Thread the copper beads on a 4" piece of wire and place around the top of the copper shaft. Trim and fold in the wire ends.
8. Attach the copper tags to the wire hearts and the 8" swirled pieces with jump rings. ❏

THE HENLEY COLLEGE LIBRARY

Party Ware

It's effortless and fun to create these beautiful pieces to dress up a party table. Color coordinate the beads with your tableware for a custom look.

CUTLERY

Supplies

- Metal long-tine (pickle) forks, spreading knives, serving spoons, 6" to 6-1/2" long
- 15" buss wire per utensil
- Glass E beads, 6 per utensil
- Masking tape
- Wire cutters
- Needlenose pliers
- Hammer
- Anvil or other hard surface

Instructions

1. Using the swirl pattern as a guide, bend the end of the wire.
2. Hammer the swirl pattern *only* to flatten.
3. Adjust the wire swirl on the utensil handle as shown in the photo and tape to hold.
4. Thread six glass beads on the end of the wire. Wrap the wire diagonally around the handle, adjusting the beads as you wrap so they sit on the front of the handle, one in each coil.
5. Finish the wire by wrapping a tight coil at the top. Trim away any excess wire. Remove the tape. ❏

Continued on page 50

PATTERNS

48

Continued from page 48

WIRE PICKS

These quick-to-make picks can be used in a variety of ways on your table. The filigree or heart designs can hold hors d'oeuvres or olives, pickles, or a slice of lime in cocktails. The swirl design could also be used to hold a card that identifies cheese or pate on a tray or as a placecard holder with an after-dinner chocolate as its base.

Patterns appear on page 48.

Supplies

- Buss wire, 8" per pick
- Glass E beads, 3 to 4 per pick
- 1 large silver crimp bead per pick
- Wire cutters
- Needlenose pliers
- Hammer
- Anvil or other hard surface

Instructions

1. Using the patterns as guides, bend the ends of the wire pieces.
2. Hammer the patterned ends *only* to flatten.
3. Thread glass beads and a crimp bead on the end of each wire. Squeeze the crimp bead with the pliers to hold the glass beads securely on the wire.
4. Trim the end of the wire at an angle for a sharp, pointed end. ❏

MARTINI GLASS

Metal martini and wine glasses are easy to find in kitchenware stores. Decorate them with wire and beads to match your party ware.

Pattern appears on page 48.

Supplies

- Metal martini glass, 6-1/2" tall
- Buss wire on a roll or spool
- Glass E beads, 10 to 12 per glass
- Wire cutters
- Needlenose pliers
- Masking tape
- Hammer
- Anvil or other hard surface

Instructions

1. Working off the roll of buss wire and using the pattern as a guide, make a swirl at the end of the wire and hammer to flatten.
2. Position the swirl at the top of the stem and tape to hold.
3. Thread 10 to 12 glass beads onto the end of the wire and wrap the wire diagonally around the handle, adjusting the beads as you wrap so they sit on the front of the stem, one in each coil.
4. Finish by wrapping the wire in a tight coil at the bottom of the stem just above the base. Trim away any excess wire. Remove the tape. ❏

Stamped Bookmarks

These colorful bookmarks are a perfect way to use beads and fibers left over from other projects. You can substitute any rubber stamp design of the appropriate size.

Supplies

- Medium-weight pewter metal sheet
- Rubber stamps with words, e.g., "INSPIRE," "CREATE"
- Ink pad for stamping on metal – Purple
- 1/8" silver eyelets
- 24 gauge beading wire
- Decorative fibers in purple hues
- Glass and silver metal beads, various types, colors, and sizes
- Brass wire brush
- Heat gun
- Awl
- Stylus
- Metal ruler
- Wire cutters
- Scissors

Instructions

Cut & Decorate the Metal:

1. Measure, mark, and cut the pewter sheet into 1-1/4" x 6" strips.
2. Burnish the metal strips with the brass wire brush to create the surface texture.
3. Stamp the metal strips with the rubber stamp(s) using purple ink.
4. Score (emboss) with a stylus and fold in each long edge 1/4".
5. Score (emboss) with a stylus and fold over one end 1/4".
6. With an awl, make a hole in the folded end of each metal strip. Insert the eyelet.

Make the Tassels:

These instructions are for one tassel.

1. Cut six 8" lengths of decorative fibers and 8" of beading wire.
2. Fold the bundle of fibers over the length of beading wire, then fold the wire in half.
3. Wrap the top of the fiber bundle close to the wire with a 12" piece of fiber and knot to secure. Trim the tassel to 3-1/2".
4. Thread on a variety of glass beads on the wire.
5. Thread through the eyelet and wrap the wire around to secure. ❏

Hammered Wire Bookmarks

The flattened wire of these bookmarks is thin enough to easily slip into a book. They look especially nice when placed in books displayed in a bookcase. They are a perfect gift for the avid readers on your list and a nice addition to a book gift.

Supplies

For one bookmark:

- Medium (3/16") soft aluminum armature wire, 8" per bookmark
- Metal label charm, mini metal tag, silver charm
- Silver jump ring
- Metal glue
- Wire cutters
- Needlenose pliers
- Awl
- Hammer
- Anvil or other hard surface

Instructions

These instructions are for one bookmark.

1. Using the pattern as a guide, bend the wire.
2. Hammer the end of the wire flat, hammering to flatten the wire less and less toward the top hooked end.
3. Hammer the very end of the hook piece to flatten. In this flattened end, use an awl to make a small hole.
4. Glue a charm to the middle of the label charm. Let dry until cured.
5. With a jump ring, attach the label charm and a mini tag to the hole in the hooked end of the bookmark. ❑

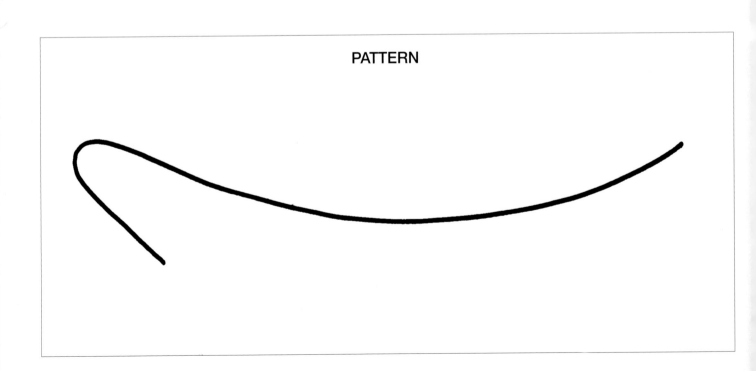

PATTERN

Copper Accented Frame

This frame was decorated with embossed copper squares, copper mesh, and different widths of copper tape for a striking modern look. Stain and varnish an unfinished flat wooden frame yourself or buy a finished frame for the base.

Supplies

- Flat wooden frame, 10" x 10" with a 3-3/4" opening
- Medium or lightweight gauge copper metal sheeting
- Embossing tools and texture plates for a variety of motifs
- Copper mesh – Fine and 1/8" diamond patterned
- Copper tape – 1/4", 1/2", and 1/8" wide
- Double-sided tape
- Scissors
- Heat gun
- Photo or mirror cut to fit frame opening

Instructions

1. Cut the copper sheet into fifteen 1" squares.
2. Emboss four squares using the embossing patterns provided.
3. Emboss three squares with textures, using texture plates or embossing wheels. Leave the remaining eight squares plain.
4. Cut the fine metal mesh into two 1" squares and one 1-1/2" square.
5. Cut the diamond patterned mesh into one 1" square and two 1-1/2" squares.
6. With the heat gun, heat the copper sheeting and mesh squares to change the color of the copper to a variety of hues. Let cool before handling.
7. Using the project photo as a guide, use double-stick tape to adhere the squares to the frame. Place some smaller copper sheet squares on the larger mesh squares to conceal the tape.
8. Add short and long pieces of the different widths of copper tape. Make a border around the frame opening with 1/8" tape and a border around the outer edges with 1/4" tape.
9. Place a photo or mirror in the frame. ❑

PATTERNS

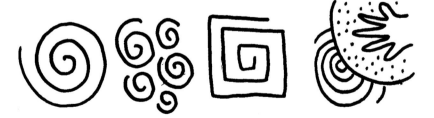

55

Romantic Cornucopia

This elegant accessory can be used as a dramatic accent or to hold a bouquet of silk flowers on a hook or doorknob. The pattern can be reduced to make smaller cornucopias – use them as seasonal decorations on a tree.

Supplies

- Medium-weight brass metal sheet
- Decorative sticker and gold charm
- Gold and amber plastic beads
- Copper wire, 20 or 22 gauge
- Gold colored wire, 20 or 22 gauge
- Wire cutters
- Metal cutters
- Ruler
- Small embossing tool
- Tracing or embossing wheel
- Epoxy glue
- Masking tape
- Gold brads
- Awl
- Embossing mat
- Tracing paper

Instructions

Make & Join the Panels:

1. Trace the pattern on tracing paper. Tape the pattern to the metal sheet and place on an embossing mat. Using the embossing tool and ruler, emboss the pattern lines four times on the brass sheet to make the four sides of the cornucopia.
2. Using metal cutters, cut out the pattern pieces from the metal sheet.
3. Turn down the top edge of each piece and burnish to form a tight fold.
4. Using a ruler and an embossing wheel or a tracing wheel, emboss the decorative border around the side edges of the four panels.
5. Using the edge of the ruler as a guide, fold just outside the embossed border to create the tabs for attaching the panels together.
6. The four panels are attached together by making four holes down the seams using an awl and attaching them together with gold brads. Mark and make all the holes before attaching the panels together.

Decorate:

1. Following instructions in the Basic Techniques section, twist the copper and gold wires together. Cut into four 20" lengths and one 5" length.
2. With epoxy glue, attach the twisted wire pieces along the panel seams, leaving a piece of wire extending 2" at the bottom of each

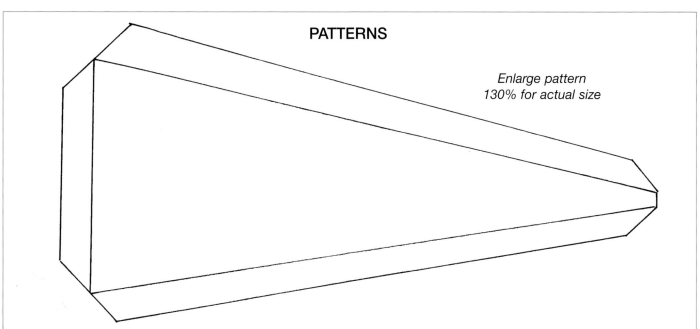

PATTERNS

Enlarge pattern 130% for actual size

panel pair and letting the rest of the wire extend above the top to create the hanger. Use masking tape to hold the wire in place while the glue cures.

3. Thread two gold beads on each piece of wire at the top. Fold the 5" piece of twisted wire in half to form a loop. Bundle it with the tops of the wires. Wrap the ends of the hanger with the other twisted wires with copper wire as shown in the photo. Form a curve in the end of each piece of twisted wire.

4. Thread a large amber bead on a 4" piece of copper wire and fold in half. Thread three or four gold beads over both wires. Attach to the bottom of the cornucopia by twisting around the ends of the twisted wires. Form a curve in the end of each piece of twisted wire.

5. Choose the panel you'd like to be the front of the cornucopia. Add a charm and a decorative sticker to that panel. ❏

Candle Snuffer

This simple snuffer design is the perfect addition when giving a gift of candles! You can vary the look of the snuffer by using different types of metal sheeting and bead colors.

Use a heavier weight metal sheet so the cone won't bend or become misshapen with use, and choose only metal or glass beads so the snuffer will be able to withstand the heat of the candle flame.

Supplies

- Heavyweight (30 gauge) tin metal sheet
- 1/4" aluminum armature wire, 7"
- Thin (1/16") aluminum armature wire, 10"
- 3 fluted silver beads, two 8mm, one 12mm
- 3 small silver brads
- Wire cutters
- Pliers
- Awl
- Hammer
- Metal cutters
- 300 grit sandpaper
- Tracing paper
- Embossing mat
- Stylus

Instructions

Make the Cone:

1. Trace the pattern on tracing paper and tape to the tin metal sheet.
2. Place the tin on an embossing mat and score the pattern lines on the tin sheet.
3. Punch the holes where indicated with an awl.
4. Cut out the cone from the metal. Sand all edges smooth.
5. Form a cone by lining up the holes. Secure with brads.

Assemble:

1. Cut the ends of the 1/4" armature wire at an angle and sand smooth.
2. Make a tiny loop at the end of the thin armature wire and thread on a small bead. (The loop prevents the bead from slipping off the wire.)
3. Thread the wire through the top of the shaped cone and thread on another small bead.
4. Evenly twist the thin armature wire around the thicker wire piece.
5. At the end of the thinner wire, thread on the large bead. Form a tiny loop to hold the bead in place. ❏

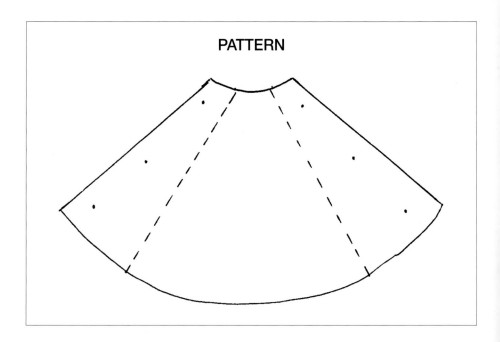

PATTERN

Copper Bulletin Board

This vivid design uses metal for a decorative border and as a pocket to hold cards or notices. You can vary the look with different papers and metal colors. TIP: Choose a decorative paper with a simple pattern for the background so the board won't look too busy.

Supplies

- Metal-edge white board, 15-1/2" x 23"
- Medium-weight copper metal sheet
- 5 mini copper brads
- 5 to 6 bottle caps
- 1" round stickers (designed to fit in bottle caps)
- Black mini clips
- Round magnets, 3/4" diameter
- Copper tape, 1/8" wide and 1/2" wide
- Double-sided tape
- 2 sheets decorative scrapbook paper, 12" square
- Permanent black marker
- Black metallic wax paste
- Epoxy glue
- Ruler

Instructions

Place the Paper:

1. Measure and mark the middle of the white board. With double sided tape, attach sheets of decorative paper to the board, joining them in the middle and leaving a 1-3/4" space at the top and bottom of the board. (The paper will overhang the edge slightly.)
2. Cut five 12" pieces of 1/8" copper tape. Attach one piece of tape to the paper where the pieces meet. Attach the rest of the tape pieces to the board, spacing them evenly.

Add the Metal Borders:

1. For the bottom metal border, cut a 3-1/2" x 24" piece of copper sheet. Crumple the metal and smooth flat. Score and fold over a 1/2" flap at top edge.
2. Position the strip at the bottom of the board, centering and marking the edges. Mark the places where the copper tape meets the copper strip and remove the strip from the board. Apply double-sided tape to back of the strip aligning it with the marks. (This will make the pockets in the copper strip that will match the copper tape strips on the paper.)
3. Place a copper brad on the copper strip at the top of each tape piece. (These are decorative and mark where you will need to burnish the tape.)
4. Re-position the copper strip across bottom of the board, securing it with the double-sided tape pieces that form the pockets. Burnish over the tape to secure. Fold the metal over the edges, trimming at the corners to fit.
5. For the top border, cut a 5" x 24" strip of copper sheet. Crumple the metal and smooth flat. Score and fold over a 1/2" flap at the bottom edge, then fold over 1/2" again to make a

thick folded flap. (This flap can be used to hold notices with black mini clips.)
6. Attach the copper strip to the top of the board with double sided tape. Fold the metal over

the edges of the board and trim at the corners to fit.

Finish:

1. Apply 1/2" wide copper tape to finish all the edges of the board.

2. Highlight the crumpled texture of the copper border strips with black metallic wax. Be careful! Don't get any wax on the paper.

3. Create magnets by flattening the bottle caps and adding the round stickers. Glue the magnets to the backs of the bottle caps with epoxy glue. ❑

Diamond Penny Ornaments

These were dubbed "diamond penny" ornaments in England because the large copper penny coins were used as templates for the pieces. The circles were folded into triangles to form a three-dimensional diamond shape with four identical sides. They were first made of paper, but using metal sheeting transforms them to bright, gleaming ornaments that can be embossed or textured.

The examples in the photo show only a few ideas of what you can do with this pattern. Follow the Basic Instructions and feel free to create your own variations – mix the metal colors, add additional beads, or change the size of the pattern, for example.

Double-sided tape holds the ornament together quite well, but if you wish a stronger bond, use an awl to make a hole in each flap and attach with brads as well as with tape.

These paper pieces are examples of how the pattern pieces are put together to form the ornament. The photos of the paper pieces show the front and the back of the ornament.

Basic Supplies
- Double-sided tape
- Small brads
- Medium-weight metal sheet
- Embossing tool
- Embossing mat
- Texture plates
- Decorative beads
- 24 gauge wire
- Tracing paper
- Masking tape

Basic Instructions

1. Trace the pattern onto paper and tape to the metal sheet. Score and cut eight pattern pieces for each ornament.
2. Trim the edges of the two side flaps as indicated on the pattern.
3. *Options:* Emboss or add texture to the triangle shapes and/or color them.
4. To construct the ornament, fold all edges on the scored lines. Using double-sided tape, attach four of the triangle pieces together at the sides. Repeat with the other four pieces to form two pyramid shapes.
5. *Option:* If adding beads to the corners of your ornament, add two lengths of wire corner to corner in the middle of the ornament.
6. With tape, join the top and bottom pyramid shapes together.

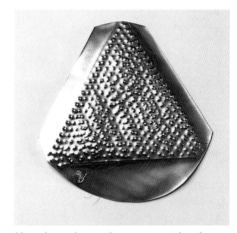

Here is a piece of copper cut by the pattern and textured. When working with metal, trim off some of the tab to remove extra bulk for folding.

7. Thread a piece of wire from the top to the bottom of the ornament to create the hanger. Add beads and make a loop or a swirl at the top and bottom to secure.
8. *Option:* If adding beads to the corners, thread beads on the wire and loop or curl the wire to hold. ❑

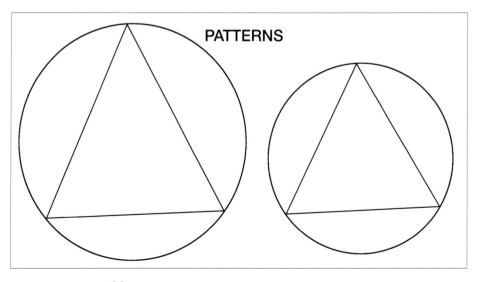

PATTERNS

BRASS & COPPER DIAMOND PENNY ORNAMENT

1. From medium-weight brass metal sheet, cut four 2-1/2" circles. Emboss with a texture plate and highlight with red metallic wax paste.
2. From medium-weight copper metal sheet, cut four 2-1/2" circles. Don't decorate them.
3. Construct the ornament with two 4" pieces of 24-gauge copper wire in the middle of the pyramid shapes. Thread a 6" piece of copper wire from the top to the bottom of the ornament.
4. Thread on a large amber bead on the wire at the bottom and top of the ornament, making loops to secure and form the hanger.
5. Thread two clear copper beads on each corner wire and swirl the wire to secure. ❏

SILVER FILIGREE DIAMOND PENNY ORNAMENT

1. From medium-weight pewter metal sheet, cut eight 2-1/2" circles.
2. Leave four pattern pieces plain. Add a silver floral brad charm to the center of each plain triangle. Emboss the remaining four pieces using a filigree texture plate.
3. Construct the ornament, alternating plain and textured sections. Thread thin (1/16") aluminum wire through the top and bottom of the ornament.
4. Thread silver fluted beads on the top and bottom wire pieces. Swirl and loop the wire ends to hold the beads securely. ❏

COPPER DIAMOND PENNY ORNAMENT

1. From medium-weight copper metal sheet, cut eight 2" circles.
2. Emboss texture on the pieces using a variety of tools and texture plates.
3. Heat each embossed piece with a heat gun to change the color of the copper.

4. Construct the ornament with two 4" pieces of 24-gauge copper wire in the middle of the pyramid shapes. Thread a 6" piece of copper wire from the top to the bottom of the ornament.
5. Thread red and copper-colored beads on the corners and bottom and top of the ornament. Make loops to secure the beads and form the hanger. ❏

Charmed Mirrors

These mirrors are decorated with a fun saying embossed on a metal banner and metal charms. The mirrors are easy to find at craft stores and come in a variety of shapes and sizes. You can display them on a wire easel or hang them on a wire or ribbon hanger.

Basic Supplies

- Mirror, 5"
- Medium-weight metal sheet
- Charms
- Metal bullion *optional*
- Metal cutters
- Embossing tools – Fine-tip embosser, embossing wheel
- Embossing mat
- Tracing wheel
- Metal glue
- Tracing paper

Basic Instructions

1. Trace the banner pattern and saying pattern on tracing paper.
2. Tape the pattern to the metal and place on an embossing mat. Trace the pattern on the metal with a fine-tip embosser.
3. Cut out the banner 1/4" from the embossed lines. Fold over all the edges of the banner.
4. Using a tracing wheel, emboss the edge the banner with a dotted line.
5. Tape the saying pattern to the banner piece. Place on an embossing mat. Trace the saying on the metal, using a fine-tip embosser.
6. Add a texture to the banner, using an embossing wheel. Be careful not to run the wheel over the lettering.
7. Fold the banner piece to wrap

Happily Ever After Oval Mirror

Use copper metal sheeting for the banner and a 5" x 7" oval mirror with a fluted beveled edge. Embellish with gold-colored cherubs and angel wing charms and rub with red metallic wax paste so they match the copper banner. Since the mirror came with two holes drilled in the top, I threaded gold metallic ribbon through the holes and tied it in a bow to form the hanger.

along the bottom of the mirror. Fold and shape the ends.

8. Arrange the charms on the mirror. Glue the banner and the charms to the mirror with metal glue.

9. *Option:* Form a looped bow with stretched bullion. Fold and glue to the banner for extra sparkle. ❏

You Look Marvelous Hexagonal Mirror

Use pewter sheeting for the banner and add silver oak leaf, acorn, and oak branch charms. Make a wire hanger by twisting two 8" lengths of buss wire together in the middle. Place on the back of the mirror and bend the wire ends over to the front of the mirror tightly. Form the wire ends into swirls to hold the mirror securely.

Once Upon a Time Round Mirror

Use brass sheeting for the banner and embellish with gold-colored crown, castle, and leaf wreath charms. Highlight the embossing with red metallic wax paste. *Optional:* Make an easel to hold the mirror from 24" of 19-gauge brass wire.

Charmed Mirrors

Once upon a time...

Instructions on page 64

PATTERNS

*Enlarge pattern
110% for actual size*

You look marvelous!

Queen for a day

Happily ever after...

Mirror, Mirror...

Dreams do come true...

...and she lived happily ever after

Beverage Can Angels

These cute folk art cherubs are made from metal recycled from aluminum beverage cans. The colored heart and star embellishments are cut from colored areas on the outside of the cans; the right sides of the silvery angels are from the inside surface of the cans.

Supplies

- Aluminum beverage cans, cut and cleaned to make a flat piece about 3-1/2" x 6-1/2", one for each angel
- Embossing mat
- Embossing tools – Paper stump, medium and small ball embossers
- Metal cutters
- Fine sandpaper
- Steel point

Instructions

These instructions are for one angel.

1. Working on a flat, hard surface, trace the angel and heart or star patterns on the metal.
2. Cut out the angel and heart or star with metal cutters. Cut a small (1/4") slit in the top of the wings and between the arms as indicated on the pattern.
3. Remove any sharp edges or burrs by sanding the edges lightly.
4. Emboss the back of the angel with the paper stump to gently form the design outlines. Working on the embossing mat, use embossing tools to add the wing and hair details.
5. Emboss the heart or the star piece from the back of the metal with the colored side on the front.
6. For the hanger, cut a strip of metal 1-1/2" x 1/8". Form the strip into a loop and insert the ends in the slit at the top of the wings. Fold up the metal strip on the back to hold in place.
7. Place the heart or star in the cut slit on the arms. ❏

PATTERNS

Repousse Trio

These little landscapes were created using the pencil crayon repousse technique. Other sources for designs you could use for this technique include coloring books and copyright-free pattern books.

THE HENLEY COLLEGE LIBRARY

Supplies

- Matte black metal sheets
- Watercolor pencils – Light green, medium green, dark green, light blue, purple, white, brick red, ochre
- Acrylic stain – Dark brown
- Clear matte spray varnish
- 3 unfinished wooden frames, 5" square with 3" square openings
- Filigree metal charms and copper embellishments
- 300 grit sandpaper
- Metal glue
- Tracing paper

Instructions

1. Stain the frames. Let dry. Sand to lightly distress the edges.
2. Glue the copper embellishments on the frames with metal glue.
3. Cut pieces of metal sheet to fit the frame openings.
4. Trace the patterns on tracing paper.
5. Following the instructions for Colored Pencil Repousse in the Basic Techniques section, color and emboss the designs on the black matte metal pieces.
6. Spray the panels with matte varnish to set the color. Let dry.
7. Install the panels in the frames. ❏

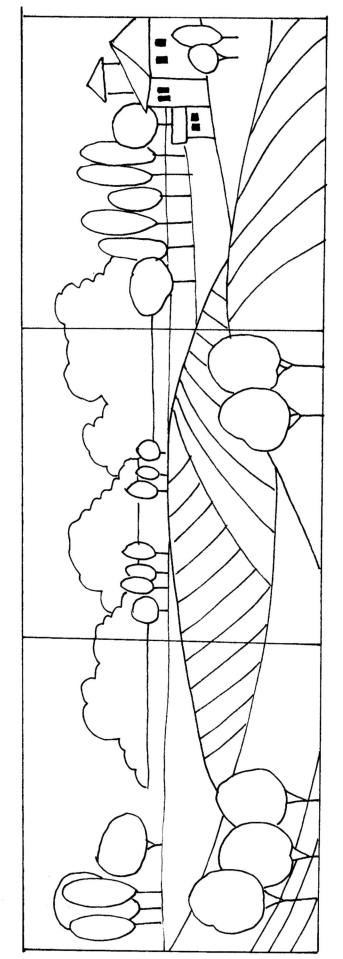

Stamped Metal Journals

These useful little booklets have embossed metal covers. Use any rubber stamp as a pattern.

Supplies

- Lightweight silver metal sheet
- Rubber stamps – Tulip and fleur de lis motifs
- Ink pads for stamping metal – Black, purple, teal, brown
- Cotton swabs
- Embossed pewter stickers
- Mini metal binder clips (4 per book)
- Charms (for ends of satin cord)
- Metal hinges (2 per book)
- Black card stock
- Cream text weight paper (for the pages)
- Mat board
- Black satin cord
- Embossing tools
- Embossing mat
- Double-sided tape
- Masking tape
- Epoxy glue

Basic Instructions

These instructions are for one book.

Cut the Paper:
1. Cut from mat board:
   Hinge piece of front cover – 1" x 4"
   Front cover – 3" x 4"
   Back cover – 4" x 4-1/4"
2. Cut from black paper:
   Inside front cover – 2-3/4" x 3-3/4"
   Inside back cover – 3-3/4" x 3-3/4"
   Fly leaf (first page) – 4" x 3-1/2"
3. Cut enough cream paper pages 4" x 3-1/2" to make a stack that measures approximately 1/4".

Make the Cover:
1. Cut a 5" x 6" piece of metal sheet.
2. Stamp with the black stamp pad and heat to set the ink.
3. Color to the motif, using a cotton swab and colored inkpads. Heat to set.
4. On the embossing mat, trace lightly around the stamped image using a small embossing tool.
5. Emboss the back of the image with the paper stump. Add details with small and medium embossing tools.
6. Center the stamped and embossed metal piece on the front cover board. Fold the corners at a 90-degree angle. Apply double-sided tape to the sides and fold over the long edges.
7. Add decorative texture to the metal with embossing tools.
8. Cut 1" square pewter stickers in half and press on the corners.
9. Cut a 2" x 5" piece of metal. Use it to cover the hinge mat board piece, using same technique used for the front cover piece.
10. Cut a 6" square piece of metal sheet. Cover the back cover piece.

Assemble:
1. Place the front cover and hinge piece right side down on a flat work surface with 1/4" between them. Arrange the hinges on the pieces and glue in place with epoxy glue. Tape with masking tape to secure while the glue cures.
2. Use double-sided tape to attach the inside cover pieces to the front and back covers, covering the folded metal edges and hinges.
3. Place the stack of pages on the back cover. Carefully place the front cover and hinge piece on top. Secure with binder clips.
4. Thread black satin cord through the binder clip wires on the back, then cross, bring to the front, and thread through the front clip wires. Knot to secure.
5. Tie charms on the ends of the cord. Add a drop of glue on each knot to keep it from unraveling. ❏

Tags & Labels

Metal tags and labels make charming additions to your handmade cards and scrapbook pages. You can also use them to adorn plain items – they make exceptional additions to decorative accessories and gifts. Rubber stamps make great patterns.

Basic Supplies

- Medium-weight pewter metal sheets
- Rubber stamps
- Ink pad for stamping on metal
- Embossing mat
- Embossing tools

Basic Instructions

Follow the instructions in the Basic Techniques section for embossing and stamping to make the labels and tags.

TIP: For small tags and labels with an embossed edge, first trace the tag shape, using a template. Then trim the metal sheet around the embossed edge.

GIFT TAGS

Patterns appear on page 76.

When making tags, it's a good idea to pierce a hole and install an eyelet for extra strength. Beads can be added as embellishments – simply thread beading wire through the eyelet and add glass beads. On the last bead, thread one piece wire back through the bead and pull tight to secure. The "Cheers" tag was burnished with a brass wire brush; the "GREETINGS" tag was heated to alter the copper color.

JAR LABELS

Shiny metal labels make great accents for herb and spice jars. An olive sprig stamp was used as the pattern for the embossed tops of the flip-top jars. The image was stamped on the back, embossed, and colored with stamp pad inks, using cotton swabs. Labels for the contents were pierced.

See page 102 for instructions and page 103 for patterns.

DECORATIVE LABELS

Decorative labels can also be used to embellish plain household objects – be sure to attach them with epoxy glue for a washable bond. A rubber stamp was used as a pattern for the oval label on the metal wine glass; a daisy stamp, black ink from an ink pad, and 1/4" silver tape were used to accent a simple glass vase.

73

Eek! Journal

A plain coil-bound journal was made extraordinary with the addition of a bright, embossed metal cover. Use this technique to add your own custom saying or design to a notebook cover.

Pattern appears on page 76.

Supplies

- Coil-bound notebook with blank pages, 8" x 6"
- Lightweight silver metal sheet, 8" x 7"
- Mat board, 6-1/2" x 5"
- Dimensional paint (any color)
- Transparent glass paint – Bright red
- 4 silver metal charm tags
- 4 jump rings
- 4 number stickers (for the year)
- Rick-rack and narrow ribbons, 10" lengths – Silver, red, black
- Metal lanyard clip
- Sticky glue
- Decorative edge scissors – Pinking edge
- Embossing tools
- Tracing paper
- Transfer paper

Instructions

1. Trace the pattern and transfer to the mat board piece.
2. Following the instructions in the Basic Techniques section for Dimensional Repousse, go over the pattern lines with dimensional paint. Let dry completely.
3. Coat the surface lightly with sticky glue. Let dry.
4. Place the metal sheet on the mat board and emboss lightly to reveal the lettering. Refine the embossing by tracing around all the letters with a small embossing tool.
5. With glass paint, fill in the large letters. Let dry.
6. Trim the metal around the mat board with pinking scissors.
7. Attach the metal-covered mat board to the front of the notebook with double-sided tape. Rub down the cut edges firmly.
8. Add number stickers to the metal charms and attach the charms to the coils with jump rings.
9. Fold the 10" pieces of ribbon and rick-rack in half and thread them through the lanyard clip to make the tassel. Wrap black satin cord around the neck of the tassel and knot to secure. Trim the end of each piece of trim at an angle. Clip the tassel to the top of the coil binding. ❏

Tags & Labels

Instructions appear on page 72.

PATTERNS

THANK YOU

Joy

Cheers

GREETINGS

Peace

EEK! Journal

Instructions appear on page 74.

PATTERNS

Labyrinth Coasters

Instructions appear on page 78.

PATTERNS

Labyrinth Coasters

Labyrinths, which have been used for centuries as tools for prayer and meditation, are symbols that represent a journey. I designed these labyrinth coasters using ancient patterns and copper metal for a primeval feeling. Use them as tabletop accessories or when, contemplating a new project, trace the paths with your finger.

Patterns appear on page 77.

Supplies

- 4" wooden tiles (or use 4" ceramic tiles with a smooth or slightly textured surface)
- Lightweight copper metal sheeting, 5" square for each coaster
- Double-sided tape
- Dimensional paint (any color)
- Tracing paper
- Transfer paper
- Thin cork sheets
- Sticky glue
- White craft glue
- Embossing tools
- Fine abrasive pad

Labyrinth or Maze?

Labyrinths and mazes are often confused. A maze is a puzzle to be solved with twists, turns, and blind alleys. Navigating a maze is a left-brain task that requires logic and analytical activity to find the correct path. The journey through a labyrinth is a right-brain task that helps encourage creativity and imagery.

Instructions

1. Trace the labyrinth patterns and transfer to the coasters with transfer paper.
2. Following the instructions for Dimensional Repousse in the Basic Techniques section, go over the pattern lines with dimensional paint. Let dry completely. TIP: For thicker lines, apply paint on the pattern lines and fill in.
3. Coat the surface lightly with sticky glue. Let dry.
4. Place the metal sheet over the coaster and rub lightly with an embossing tool to reveal the pattern.
5. Refine the embossing by pressing around the design with a small embossing tool.
6. Fold the metal over the edges of the tiles and secure with double-sided tape.
7. Rub the top of the embossed metal with a fine abrasive pad for surface contrast.
8. Cut out 4" x 4" pieces of thin cork sheet.
9. Glue the cork to the bottoms of the coasters with white craft glue. Weight with large, heavy books while the glue cures. ❏

Embossed Silver Frame

Think of words to describe a photo and emboss them on metal to make this customized frame. You can use the patterns provided or generate lettering on a computer using a simple sans serif font in sizes from 60 to 80 points. TIP: Use the font formatting key to create loose character spacing – this makes it easier to read the lettering.

Pattern appears on page 82.

Supplies

- Wooden frame, 12" x 12" with a 4-1/2" x 6-1/2" opening
- Lightweight silver metal sheet
- Silver charms
- Silver metal tape, 1/4" wide
- 1/8" patterned wire mesh
- Dimensional paint (any color)
- Tracing wheel
- Texture embossing wheels
- Hammer
- Embossing tools
- Transfer paper
- Epoxy glue
- Photo to fit frame opening
- *Optional:* Computer and printer

Instructions

1. Divide the surface of the frame into six rectangles. Use the project photo as a guide or create your own design.
2. Transfer a word to each rectangle, using a variety of placements (sideways, centered, offset, etc.).
3. Following the instructions in the Basic Techniques section for Dimensional Repousse, go over the pattern lines with dimensional paint. Let dry completely.
4. Coat the surface lightly with sticky glue. Let dry.
5. Cut pieces of metal sheet 1/2" larger in each dimension than the rectangular sections of the frame.
6. Place the metal pieces over the corresponding sections of the frame. On one section, use double sided tape to attach a piece of mesh (avoiding the word) before placing the metal sheet. Emboss lightly to reveal the mesh pattern on that section and the words. Emboss the rest of the words. Refine the embossing by tracing around the embossed words with a small embossing tool.
7. Burnish the metal and add hammered textures, filigree designs, or stripes with silver tape or embossing wheels to decorate each section differently.
8. Apply silver tape to cover the joints between the sections.
9. Glue charms in place with epoxy glue. Let dry.
10. Place the photo in the frame. ❑

Embossed Silver Frame

Instructions appear on page 80.

PATTERNS

JOYFUL

CHEERFUL

SPIRITED

OPTIMISTIC

SPARKLING

GENEROUS

Embossed Box Purse

Instructions appear on page 84.

PATTERN

Embossed Box Purse

An aqua metal sheet provided the base color for this embossed box purse, which is embellished with glass paints, a beaded handle, and a colorful tassel.

Pattern appears on page 83.

Supplies

- Wooden purse blank, 6-1/2" x 8", with hinges and latch
- Wire purse handle
- Handle clamps
- Lightweight colored metal sheet, 7-1/2" x 9" – Aqua
- Silver tape, 1/4" wide
- Beads – Silver, turquoise
- Acrylic rhinestones
- Acrylic craft paint – Aqua
- Clear acrylic matte varnish
- Dimensional paint (any color)
- Glass paints – Blue, green
- Sticky glue
- Embossing tools – paper stump, fine ball embosser

For the tassel:

- Metal lanyard hook
- Decorative fibers – Green, blue
- Beads – Blue, green
- Tracing paper
- Transfer paper

Instructions

1. Remove the hardware from the purse and set aside.
2. Basecoat the wooden purse, inside and out, with aqua acrylic paint. Let dry.
3. Apply a coat of matte varnish. Let dry.
4. Trace the pattern and transfer to the side of the purse.
5. Following the instructions for Dimensional Repousse in the Basic Techniques section, go over the pattern lines with dimensional paint. Let dry completely.
6. Coat the surface lightly with sticky glue. Let dry.
7. Place the metal piece over the dimensional paint and emboss lightly to reveal the pattern. Refine the embossing by tracing around the pattern with a small embossing tool.
8. Fold the metal over the edges of the purse and secure with metal tape.
9. Accent the embossed design with glass paints and use glass paint to attach the rhinestones. Let dry.
10. Reassemble purse.
11. Thread the silver and turquoise beads on the wire handle and secure the handle to the purse.
12. Make a tassel on the lanyard clip, using the fibers and beads. Attach the tassel to the purse handle. ❑

Copper Lantern

Soft, flickering candlelight shines beautifully through this copper lantern. The round metal frame, available at craft outlets, makes it easy to create your lantern.

Supplies

- Round wire lantern frame, 5-1/2" x 8"
- Black wire, 19 gauge
- Lightweight copper metal sheet
- Fine copper mesh
- Copper mesh with 1/8" diamond pattern
- Copper tape, 1/2" wide
- Copper brads with floral charm heads
- Votive or pillar candle
- Metal cutters
- *Optional:* Metal glue

Instructions

1. Cut the copper sheet into eight 8" x 1/2" strips and eight 4-1/2" x 1/2" strips.
2. Cut the fine copper mesh into eight 8" x 1/2" strips and eight 4-1/2" x 1/2" strips.
3. Use the bands provided with the wire frame to construct and hold the frame together as you work. Alternating the copper and mesh strips, attach the 8" strips to two opposite panels, folding the ends over the frame.
4. Use the shorter strips to weave over and under the longer strips, folding the ends over the wire frame.
5. Apply copper tape to the insides of the panels to frame the woven strips and hold them together.
6. Cut the copper diamond mesh to 8" x 4-1/2". Fold the top and bottom edges over the wire

frame. Apply copper tape to the inside of the panel to frame the panel and conceal the cut ends of the mesh. (The fourth panel of the frame is left open.)
7. Cut four 7" pieces of black wire. Secure to the bottom of the frame by twisting the ends around the frame to form a plat-

form for the candle.
8. Decorate the mesh panel with floral brads, pushing them through the mesh and bending the ends open. *Option:* Glue charms to the mesh with metal glue.
9. Place the candle on the wire platform. ❏

Sparkle & Smile Frame

Instructions appear on page 88.

PATTERN

Sparkle & Smile Frame

Use this embellished frame to hold a favorite photo or a mirror and greet the morning with a smile!

Pattern appears on page 87.

Supplies

- Flat wooden frame, 12" square with 4" square opening
- Acrylic craft paint – Light blue
- Aluminum mesh with 3/8" diamond pattern, 4" x 4"
- Mirror, 3" square
- Aluminum sparkle 1/8" wire mesh, 14" square
- Thin (1/16") aluminum wire
- Hammer and anvil
- Silver label charms
- Silver metal tape, 1/2" wide
- 4 silver metal corners
- Mirror mosaic pieces, squares and diamonds, in a variety of sizes
- Metal letters to spell "dance," "play," and "sing"
- Clear rhinestones, variety of shapes and sizes
- Metal glue

Instructions

1. Basecoat the frame with light blue paint. Let dry.
2. Cover the frame with sparkle mesh, folding the mesh over the outside edges and the inside opening. Fold the excess wire mesh at the corners and burnish down.
3. Tape down the mesh edges with metal tape.
4. Bend the aluminum wire to create the words, using the pattern as a guide. Hammer the wire. (See "Hammering" in the Basic Techniques section.)
5. Arrange and glue the wire words, metal letters, mirror pieces, and embellishments in place with metal glue. (You may need to weight the pieces so they lay flat on the mesh until the glue dries. TIP: Place a piece of wax paper between the frame and the weights (e.g., heavy books) to prevent the glue from sticking to the objects you're using as weights.)
6. Glue the rhinestones and metal corners in place.
7. Glue the 4" mesh square in the opening. Glue the mirror on the mesh. ❏

Brass & Bead Lantern

Brass mesh covers a wire frame to form a square lantern. Glass beads allow candle-light to shine through. To customize the look, change the bead colors. The wire frame is available at craft stores.

Supplies

Square wire frame, 4-1/2" x 8"

Square patterned brass mesh

24 gauge black wire

30 gauge gold beading wire

Glass beads, variety of shapes and sizes – Blues, greens

Metal brads with floral charm heads

Flat glass marbles, 1-1/2" and 1/2" – Greens, blues

Metal glue

Wire cutters

Metal cutters

Tea light candle in metal cup

Instructions

Use the bands that come with the wire frame to construct the frame and hold it together while you work.

1. Cut two 6" x 1-1/4" strips of mesh. Fold the mesh over the bottom rungs of the wire frame to form a platform for the tea light. Secure by using gold beading wire to stitch the strips together. Twist the ends of the wire together to finish.
2. Cut four 4-1/2" x 7" mesh panels. Use black wire to "sew" the panels to the frame at the corners, using a simple whipstitch through every other square.
3. Use a length of black wire to attach the glass beads along the top of the lantern by threading the beads on the wire and whipstitching around the frame. Twist the wire ends together to finish.
4. To decorate the front panel, glue flat marbles, beads, and floral brads in a cascading design, using the photo as a guide for placement. Let the glue cure completely.
5. Add smaller bead-and-marble designs to the side panels.
6. Place the candle on the mesh platform. ❏

THE HENLEY COLLEGE LIBRARY

Mesh Vases & Votives

Expandable wire mesh makes wonderful domed lids for jars that can be used as potpourri containers or flower vases. (The mesh dome becomes a floral frog that holds flower stems in place.) The dome shape is created by forming the mesh over a rubber ball the same diameter as the jar neck opening. Make some matching votive holders to display with your vase – you can use them as a centerpiece on your dining table.

Supplies

- Glass jars with 3" diameter necks, 3" tall (for potpourri) or 4" tall (for a vase)
- Rubber ball, 3"
- 2 round glass votive candles with straight sides, 2-3/4" tall, 2" diameter
- Expandable metal mesh with 3/8" diamond pattern
- Lightweight aluminum metal sheet
- Small silver brads
- Silver label charms
- Art stickers (for the charms)
- Awl
- Metal cutters

Vase/Jar Instructions

The dome should fit snugly but should be loose enough to be removed easily for cleaning the jar.

1. Cut a 6" square of mesh for each vase or potpourri jar.
2. Form the mesh over the rubber ball to make the dome shape. Trim away the excess mesh at the bottom so the mesh shape fits loosely over the rim of the jar.
3. Cut a 11" x 1-1/2" strip of metal sheet. Fold in the long edges of the strip to make a band 5/8" wide.
4. Cut a decorative sticker to fit inside a label charm. Set aside.
5. Attach the metal band around the bottom of the mesh dome with silver brads, spacing the brads 1" apart. Use an awl to make a hole and push the brad through the metal band and the mesh. Attach the label charm to one brad.
6. Put the dome on the jar. ❏

Votive Instructions

These instructions are for one votive. Repeat to make additional ones.

1. Cut an 8" x 3" strip of mesh and place it around the glass votive. Fold over the wire edges to form a snug cylinder. Remove from the votive.
2. Cut a 7-1/2" x 1-1/4" strip of metal sheet. Fold in the long edges of the strip to form a band 5/8" wide.
3. Cut a decorative sticker to fit inside a label charm. Set aside.
4. Attach the metal band around the top of the votive with silver brads, spacing the brads 1" apart. Use an awl to make a hole and push the brad through the metal band and the mesh. Attach the label charm to one brad.
5. Place the metal cylinder over the glass votive. ❏

Crown Jewels Box

A regal paint color and an embossed panel make this a perfect box to hold the jewels of your little princess!

Supplies

- Wooden box, 7-1/4" square, 3" tall, with a 6" square inset
- Lightweight aluminum metal sheet
- 30 gauge tin, 6" square
- Embossing template – Border design
- Embossing tools
- Piercing tools – Piercing point, hammer, and particle board base
- Acrylic craft paint – Metallic purple
- Glass paints – Blue, purple
- Purple suede paper
- Dense foam sponge
- Metal glue
- White craft glue
- Silver metal tape
- Rhinestone letters
- Ribbon buckle label
- Acrylic rhinestones

Instructions

1. Basecoat the outside and the inside sides of the wooden box with metallic purple. Let dry.
2. Line the inside top and bottom of the box with suede paper cut to fit. Glue in place with white craft glue.
3. Pierce the crown design into the tin piece, following the piercing instructions in the Basic Techniques section.
4. Color the metal inside the crown by sponging on thin coats of blue and purple glass paints, using a dense foam sponge. Let dry.
5. Glue the pierced tin panel on the box top with metal glue. Let dry and cure.
6. Emboss four 6" metal borders, using the border embossing template on lightweight aluminum sheet. Trim the embossed borders to fit and glue around the pierced tin panel.
7. Attach the metal tape around the bottom of the box. Attach the ribbon buckle label on the front side.
8. Attach rhinestone initials inside the buckle label.
9. Glue rhinestones on the crown to add extra sparkle. ❑

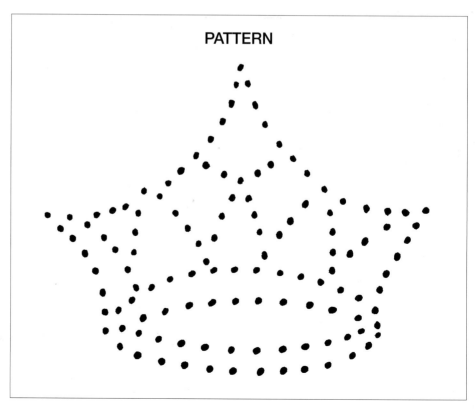

PATTERN

Pierced Plate

Purchased metal plates, trays, and buckets can be pierced with designs. Because the back of a pierced plate will be rough and sharp, cover it with a thin foam sheet to protect your table.

Supplies

- Metal plate
- Piercing tools – Point punch and chisel
- Piercing mat (See "Work Surface for Piercing" in the Equipment section.)
- Thin foam sheeting
- Scissors
- Metal glue
- Tracing paper
- Masking tape

Instructions

1. Trace the pattern on tracing paper. Tape the pattern so it's centered on the plate.
2. Following the Metal Piercing instructions in the Basic Techniques section, pierce the design, starting in the center of the plate and working out to the edge.
3. Cut a circle of thin foam sheeting to fit the bottom of the plate. Glue on the bottom of the plate using metal glue. ❑

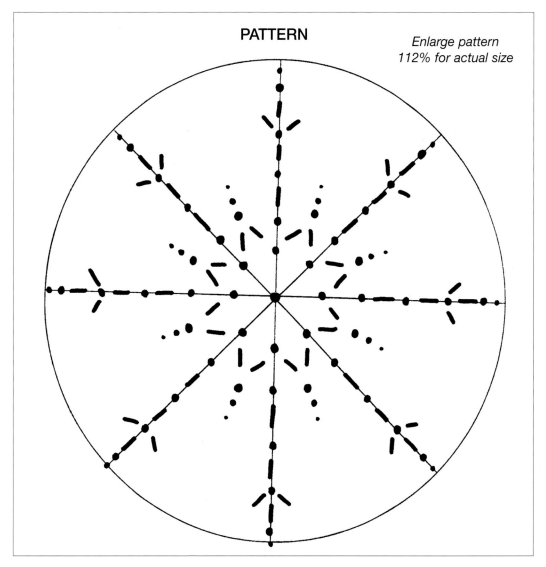

PATTERN

Enlarge pattern 112% for actual size

Party Lights

These bright, shiny buckets can be used to hold tea light candles, candies, or party favors. Customize the handles to fit the occasion ("Happy Birthday," "Congrats," "Welcome," "Rejoice") or use them as placecards by creating name handles.

Supplies

- Tin buckets, 3" high, 3" diameter
- Silver bullion wire
- Thin (1/16") aluminum armature wire on a spool
- Piercing tools – Point punch and chisel
- Old towel
- Pliers

Instructions

1. Remove the original handles from the buckets. Fill the buckets with water and place in the freezer overnight.
2. Following the Metal Piercing instructions in the Basic Techniques section, pierce a simple design on the front of the bucket. When finished, remove the ice by placing the bucket under hot water. Dry the bucket.
3. Stretch and wrap the bullion around top of bucket, twisting the ends to hold.
4. Use your own handwriting to make patterns for the word handles.

This photo shows how beautifully the light glimmers through the pierced design of these festive little bucket candleholders.

5. Working from the spool, form the wire into words. Use pliers to pinch the wire so the words can be read easily.

6. Trim the end of the wire. Place the ends of the handle in the bucket's brackets. Pinch the wire with pliers to hold.

7. Stretch some bullion slightly and form two looped bows for each bucket. Twist the centers to hold, then fold the bows in half and place in the handle bracket holes. Press with your fingers to secure. ❏

Old World Spice Cabinet

This curved-front wooden cabinet was designed to hold a tin tile, but you could create the same effect on a plain cabinet by gluing on a painted and decoupaged tin panel. I chose this decorative paper for its old world look, but you could use any decorative paper that complements your home decor.

Fill the cabinet with glass jars that have the same painted rust finish on their lids and embossed metal labels.

Supplies

- Spice cabinet, 13-1/2" x 12" x 5-1/2" deep
- Glass spice jars with metal lids, 1-1/2" x 4"
- Tin tile, 12" x 12"
- Medium-weight pewter metal sheet
- Acrylic antiquing medium – Dark brown
- Metal paints – Burnt sienna, dark brown
- Metallic paste wax – Turquoise
- Painting sponges
- Scrapbooking paper with renaissance art motifs
- Decoupage medium
- 300 grit sandpaper
- Metal copper filigree pieces
- Small brass finishing nails
- Metal glue
- Metal cutters
- Paper trimmer
- Stylus
- Embossing mat
- Tracing paper and fine-tip marker

Continued on page 102

Old World Spice Cabinet *Continued from previous page.*

Instructions for Spice Cabinet

1. Stain the inside and outside of wooden cabinet with dark brown antiquing medium. Let dry.
2. With sandpaper, lightly sand the center panel of the tin tile.
3. Following the instructions in the Basic Techniques section, create a rusted metal painted finish on the front of the tile.
4. With a paper trimmer, cut the scrapbook paper into one 3-1/2" square and twelve 1-1/2" squares.
5. Using the photo as a guide, decoupage these squares on the center panel of the tin tile, leaving a small (1/8") space between the paper pieces.
6. Using small finishing nails, attach the metal filigree pieces to the front of the cabinet and the inside shelves. ❏

Instructions for Spice Jars

1. Paint the lids of the spice jars with the rusted metal finish you used on the tin panel. Let dry.
2. Using the pattern provided, cut out oval labels for the jars from medium-weight pewter sheet. Use the tracing wheel to made a border on the outer edge of each label.
3. Using a metal label as a template, draw the shape on tracing paper, making one label for each jar. Write the names of your herbs and spices on the paper with a fine-tip marker.
4. Place the label on an embossing pad with your written label pattern face down over the label. Trace over your writing with a stylus to emboss the name of the herb or spice. Repeat the process to emboss each label.
5. Glue the labels to the jars with metal glue. ❏

Pierced Labels

You can also make metal labels with pierced letters. I like to use medium-weight pewter metal sheet for the labels and a pushpin or small awl to pierce the holes. An easy way to make patterns for piercing is to type the words on a computer, using a simple sans serif font and a very loose character spacing. When piercing, make the holes close together so the lettering will be easy to read. Use metal glue to adhere the labels to the surface. ❏

Pierced Labels

PAPRIKA	DILL
OREGANO	GARLIC
SALT	MARJORAM
PEPPER	NUTMUG
ALLSPICE	CINNAMON
BASIL	PARSLEY
CAYENNE	ROSEMARY
CUMIN	TARRAGON
CURRY	SAGE

Blue Tin Tile Clock

A wooden frame designed to hold scrapbook pages can also frame a painted tin tile.
Adding a clock mechanism makes the tin tile a clock.

Supplies

- Tin tile with floral design, 12" square
- Wooden frame, 13-1/2" square with a 12" square opening
- Clock hands and mechanism
- 12 square-topped silver brads, 3/16"
- 4 corner charms
- Acrylic craft paints – Gray, medium blue, white
- Metal paints – Medium blue, white
- 300 grit sandpaper
- Piece of wax (e.g., an old white candle)
- Metal glue
- Awl

Instructions

Paint the Frame:

1. Paint the wooden frame with one coat of gray acrylic paint. Let dry. Rub randomly with a piece of wax.
2. Brush on one coat of medium blue acrylic paint. Let dry. Rub with a piece of wax.
3. Apply a topcoat of white acrylic paint. Let dry.
4. Sand the frame. Where the wax was applied, the paint will sand off easily, revealing the bottom paint colors.

Paint the Metal Tile:

1. Basecoat the tin tile with two coats of medium blue metal paint. Let dry.
2. Sand lightly, avoiding the middle panel, to create a distressed look.
3. Dilute white metal paint with water to make a wash and lightly brush the tile surface. Wash the white paint on the corner charms. Let dry.

Finish:

1. Mark and pierce the holes to mark the clock face and center hole. Install the brads in the clock face holes.
2. Install the clock mechanism, placing the hands through the center hole.
3. Install the tile in the painted frame.
4. Glue the corner charms in the corners of the frame. ❏

Hydrangea Tile

The French words on this tin tile inspired the hydrangea bouquet. The decorated tile is mounted on a piece of foam board, trimmed with ribbons and metal embellishments, and displayed on a wire easel.

Find instructions for wire easel on page 44.

Supplies

- Tin tile with French script, 8" square
- Silver metal embellishment – Fleur de lis
- Lightweight silver metal sheet, cut into strips 1" wide
- Foam core board, 1/2 thick, 8" square
- Metal paint – Soft green
- Sepia-toned varnish
- Paper flowers and leaves *or* small silk flowers
- Thin purple ribbon
- Purple daisy trim
- 300 grit sandpaper
- Double-sided tape
- Glue gun and clear glue sticks

Instructions

1. Basecoat the tin tile with soft green metal paint. Let dry.
2. Sand the tile lightly to distress and highlight the embossed detail.
3. Attach the ribbon to the lower part of the tile with double-sided tape.
4. Glue the metal accent in place with metal glue. Let dry.
5. Attach the metal strips around the edges of the foam core board with double-sided tape, folding the metal over the edges of the foam board.
6. Glue the tile to the foam board, using the metal glue. Weight while drying with heavy books for a strong bond. Let dry completely.
7. Drip a pile of hot glue in the center of the tin tile. Let cool and harden. Hot glue the flower blossoms and leaves to this raised base.
8. Paint the flowers and leaves with sepia-toned varnish for an aged look.
9. Adhere the daisy trim to the covered edges of the foam board with metal glue. ❑

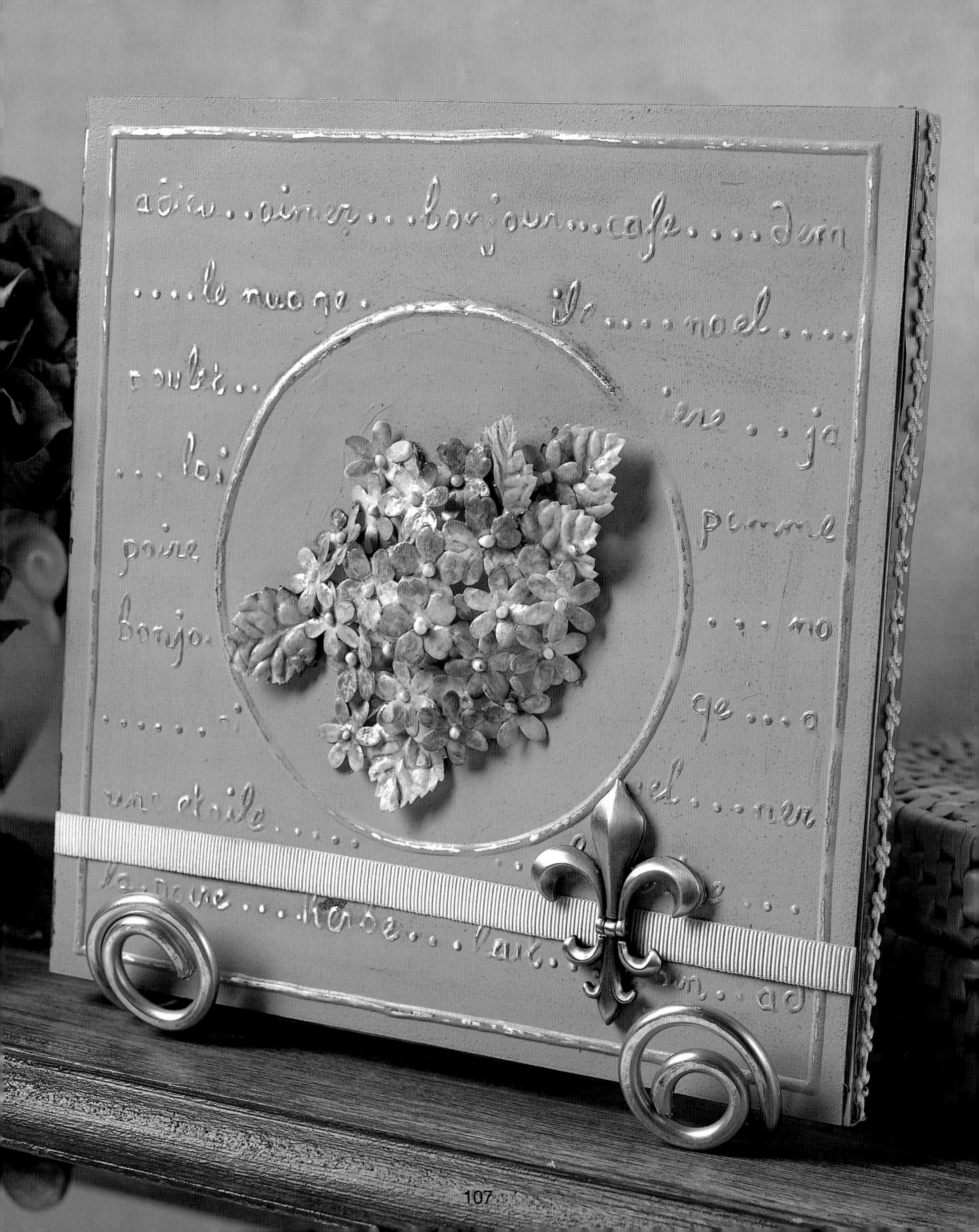
aimer...bonjour...cafe
le nuage
noel
poire
pomme
une etoile

Double Desk Frame

With small tin tiles and metal discs, you can create an old-fashioned frame to display vintage photographs. To preserve your original photographs, scan them and make prints or use photocopies.

Supplies

- 2 tin tiles, 4" square
- Black suede paper
- 2 metal discs, 2-1/2" diameter
- 2 silver hinges
- Silver brads
- Epoxy glue
- Scissors
- Photos

Instructions

1. Cut the black suede paper into two 3-3/4" squares.
2. Glue the suede paper panels to backs of the tiles.
3. Attach the brads through the holes in the hinges. (This gives a finished look to the exposed hinges.)
4. Place the tiles face down and 1/8" apart on your work surface. Glue the hinges to the backs of the tiles with epoxy glue.
5. Cut the photos to fit the discs and glue to the discs.
6. Glue the discs to fronts of the tiles with epoxy glue. ❏

THE HENLEY COLLEGE LIBRARY

Fence Post Vases

These charming metal vases, made from a tin tile, are designed to be displayed on a fence. They can hold a living plant if you stuff the bottom with moss before filling them with potting soil. To hold freshly cut flowers, cut a 6" deep corner from large plastic freezer bag to make a liner so the vase will hold the water.

Pattern appears on page 112.

Supplies

- Tin tile, 12" square (One tile makes two vases.)
- 10" buss wire
- 6 brads
- Metal paint – Soft green
- Metal cutters
- Fine embossing tool
- Ruler
- Hammer
- Awl
- 2 metal eyelets
- 2 decorative label stickers

Instructions

Assemble:

1. Mark and cut the tile in half, corner to corner, to form two triangles. (Fig. 1) Use one triangle to make each vase.
2. Following the pattern lines, score (Fig. 1) and fold in each corner 2-1/2". (Fig. 2)
3. Again following the pattern lines, mark 2-1/2" from the bottom and cut off the corner. (Fig. 1) Set this piece aside. Fold up the bottom edge 1/4".
4. Shape the metal piece into a cone shape, overlapping the back seam 1/2". (Fig. 3)
5. Mark a hole at the top and three more along the seam. (Fig. 3) Uncurl the shape and pierce all the holes with a hammer and awl.
6. Re-form the cone shape and place the brads through the lower three holes to hold the shape.
7. Mark and emboss a line 1/4" from the edge across the long edge of the cut corner piece from the bottom of the tile. Fold on the scored line and slip over the front of the cone. Burnish the metal to secure to the cone.
8. Add an eyelet to top hole to reinforce it.
9. Repeat the process with the other half of the tile to make the second vase.

Finish:

1. Basecoat the insides and outsides of the cones with two to three coats of metal paint. Let dry between coats.
2. Cut the piece of buss wire in half. Fold each piece into a loop to make a wire hanger. Thread one loop through the eyelet in each top hole. Curl the ends of the buss wire loops to hold.
3. Add a decorative label sticker to the front of each vase. ❑

Fence Post Vases

Instructions appear on page 110

PATTERN

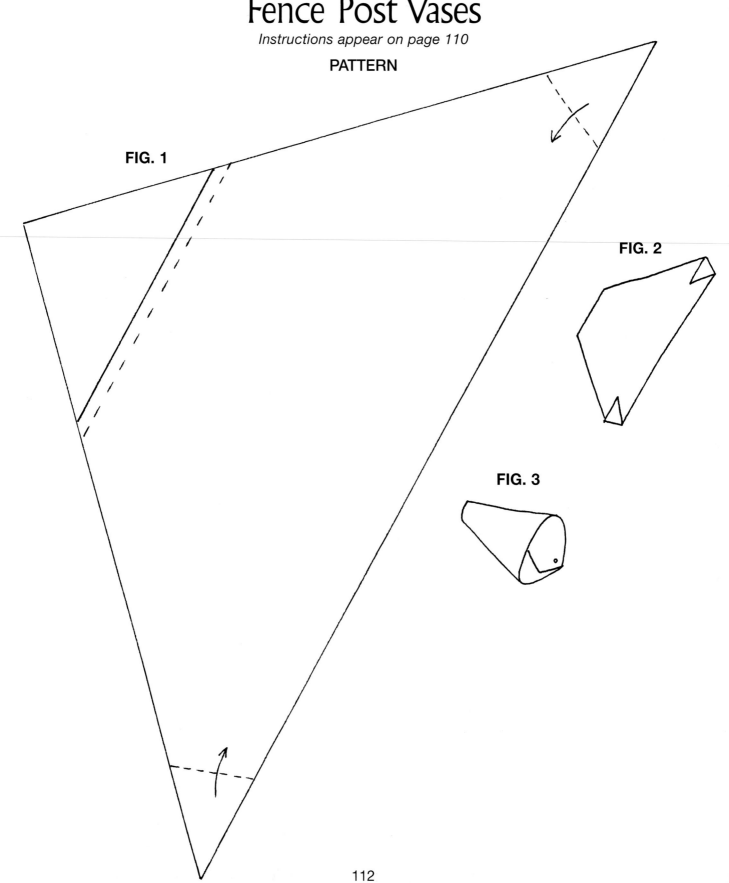

FIG. 1

FIG. 2

FIG. 3

Playing Cards Tray

Instructions appear on page 114

PATTERNS

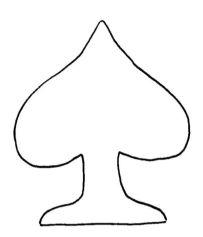

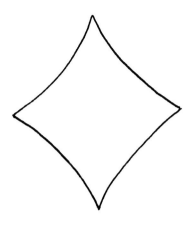

Playing Cards Tray & Coasters

This tray is made from a wooden frame designed for holding scrapbook pages. These frames are easy to find in craft and scrapbooking stores and can be used as a tray when handles are attached. Simple shapes were cut from freezer paper to create the stencils for suit motifs.

Patterns appear on page 113.

Supplies

- Tin tile with four panels, 12" square
- Wooden frame with backing, 13-1/2" square
- Acrylic craft paint – Antique ivory
- Metal paints – Ivory, red, black
- 2 silver drawer pulls
- Freezer paper
- Tracing paper
- Scissors
- Dense foam sponge
- Metal glue
- Drill and drill bit
- Pencil
- Paint brushes

Instructions

Paint:
1. Basecoat the wooden frame with antique ivory acrylic paint. Let dry.
2. Position the drawer pulls on opposite sides of the frame and mark the holes. Use a drill to drill holes. Attach the pulls to the sides of the tray with screws.
3. Dilute ivory metal paint with water and brush a wash of paint on the tin tile. Let dry.
4. Paint the inside areas of the four panels with undiluted ivory metal paint. Apply enough coats for solid coverage. Let dry between coats.

Stencil:
1. Trace the patterns for the stencils on tracing paper.
2. Cut four 6" squares from freezer paper. Create a stencil for each motif by folding the pattern in half lengthwise and folding a freezer paper square in half. Tape the folded pattern to the folded freezer paper. Follow the pattern lines to cut out the motif. Repeat with remaining motifs. Unfold to reveal the stencil.
3. Tape the stencils in the middle of each panel of the tin tile, placing the stencils shiny side up.
4. Using a dense foam sponge, apply a very thin layer of metal paint through the stencil openings. Use both red and black metal paints on each motif to shade and highlight. See the photo.
5. Glue the finished tin tile in the wooden frame with metal glue. Weight the tile while the glue cures for a strong bond. ❏

PLAYING CARD COASTERS

I found some wonderful vintage-look napkins with playing card motifs for the coasters. When you decoupage the thin printed layer of napkins over an embossed tin surface, the detail is retained. If you can't find card-theme napkins, you could use the stencils you used on the tray to decorate your coasters.

Supplies
- 4 tin tiles with embossed borders, 4" square
- 4 wooden coasters, 4" square
- Acrylic craft paint – Light ivory
- Metal paint – Light ivory
- Decoupage medium
- 300 grit sandpaper
- 16 self-adhesive cork dots (4 per coaster)
- Metal glue

Instructions
1. Basecoat the wooden coasters with light ivory acrylic paint. Let dry.
2. Lightly sand the surface of the tin tiles. Wipe away dust.
3. Paint the tin tiles with a wash of diluted light ivory metal paint.
4. Cut motifs 3-1/2" square from the napkins. Peel away the unprinted layers of paper.
5. Brush decoupage medium on the tin tiles and position a napkin motif on each one. Let dry.
6. Brush the napkin carefully with two coats of decoupage medium. Let dry completely.
7. Sand the tile lightly over the embossed border areas until the metal color shows through. Avoid sanding the decoupaged part of the tile.
8. Glue the tin tiles to the coasters with metal glue. Weight the tile while the glue cures for a strong bond. ❏

Bottle Cap Box

It's hard to imagine the beautiful design on the box top was made with bottle caps! The flattened caps are perfect for framing round stickers that are sold alongside the caps in craft stores. You can also create your own images for the caps by using a shape cutter and circle template to cut small circles from photographs or other decorative papers.

Supplies

- Square wooden box with a flat lid, 5-1/2" x 5-1/2" x 4"
- Acrylic craft paint – Black
- Clear matte finish varnish
- Decoupage medium
- Clear dimensional paint – Sepia-tone
- 4 wooden knobs, 1" diameter (for the box feet)
- 20 bottle caps, hammered flat
- 16 round stickers to fit bottle caps
- Decorative scrapbook paper
- Awl and hammer
- Small metal frame
- Small brass nails
- White craft glue
- Metal glue
- Paper trimmer or scissors

Instructions

Cover the Box:

1. Nail four bottle caps to the bottom of the box in the corners.
2. Glue on the wooden knobs for feet. Let dry.
3. Basecoat the box lid, the outside, and the inside of the box with black acrylic paint. Paint right over the bottle caps and wooden feet on the bottom of the box. Let dry.
4. Cut pieces of decorative paper to fit the sides of the box. Using decoupage medium, glue them to the box.
5. Cut a motif from paper to fit your metal frame. Decoupage the motif to the front of the box where you want the frame to be. (Use the photo as a guide for placement.)
6. Varnish the painted and decoupaged surfaces with the clear matte varnish. Let dry.

Decorate:

1. Glue the frame to the front of the box over the decoupaged motif, using metal glue.
2. Using an awl and hammer, pierce a hole in the middle of each flattened bottle cap. Nail the caps to the top of the lid in four rows of four caps each. TIP: Add a drop of metal glue under each cap before nailing for extra hold.
3. Brush the bottle caps with a wash of black paint for an aged look and wipe to leave the paint in the grooves of the caps. Let dry.
4. Glue the round stickers in each bottle cap, using white craft glue. So the stickers do not curl up while drying, press them down as they dry. Let dry completely.
5. Apply a generous amount of sepia-toned dimensional paint to the image in each bottle cap and to the front motif. (This tints the images and gives them a shiny, domed appearance.) ❑

Metal Disc Book

A little round book holds a string of photographs folded inside accordion-style. This easy design makes a unique gift.

Supplies

- 2 metal discs, 3" diameter
- Oval label charm
- 1 silver hinge
- 4 silver brads
- Decorative scrapbook paper with clock motifs and lettering
- Embossed suede paper – Burgundy
- Clock motif stickers
- Clear dimensional paint – Sepia-tone
- Burgundy satin ribbon, 1/4" wide
- Awl
- Hammer
- Photocopies of photos

Instructions

Construct the Covers:

1. Using the awl and hammer, punch holes in the metal discs to correspond with the holes in the hinge. Attach the hinge with the brads to make the round cover for the book.
2. Cut out a 2-1/2" circle from decorative paper and glue to the front cover. Add decorative stickers.
3. Glue the label charm to the middle of the front cover. Using the template that comes with the label charm, cut out a motif from the decorative paper and glue in the label. Let dry.
4. Apply a generous amount of sepia dimensional paint inside the oval label. Let dry.
5. Cut two 2-1/2" circles from the suede paper.
6. Cut two 13" pieces of ribbon. Glue one end of one ribbon to the inside of the front cover. Glue the other ribbon piece to the inside of the back cover. (These ribbon ties will hold the book closed.)
7. Glue the suede paper circles to the insides of the discs, covering the ends of the ribbon and tucking the paper under the hinge.
8. Finish each ribbon end with a small tag cut from decorative paper.

Add the Pages:

1. To make the five pages, cut ten 2-1/2" circles from decorative paper. Cut a 15" piece of ribbon.
2. Glue the two page sets, wrong sides together, with the ribbon sandwiched in between them. Let the ribbon extend beyond the pages on one end and let the last two pages cover the end of the ribbon.
3. Glue the ribbon ends to the back cover. Attach a sticker to hold the ribbon and cover the cut ends.
4. Add a sticker to decorate the inside front cover.
5. Crop and cut the photos to 2" circles and glue them on the pages. Let dry.
6. Fold up the pages, accordion-style, inside the book covers. Tie the ribbons to hold the covers closed. ❏

Metal Disc Ornaments

These ornaments, created with two metal discs, fit nicely into envelopes and travel well so they make unique holiday greeting cards. Customize them for the recipient with different decorative papers, stickers, and colors.

Supplies

For one ornament.

- 2 metal discs, 2-1/4" or 3" diameter
- 1 flattened bottle cap
- 1 round sticker, 1" diameter – design of your choice to fit inside bottle cap
- Decorative scrapbook paper
- Decoupage medium
- Circle template (or use the pattern that comes with metal discs)
- Metal stickers
- Charms
- Dimensional clear paint
- Metallic wax paste (Choose a color to match your paper.)
- Metal glue
- 22 gauge wire, 3" (to form a loop for hanging)
- Acrylic rhinestones – Various sizes, shapes, and colors
- Eyelash fibers in matching colors
- Pencil

Instructions

1. Twist the middle of the wire piece around a pencil to form a circular loop.
2. Glue the wire ends between the two metal discs with a generous amount of metal glue. Let the glue cure.
3. Cut two decorative circles from the scrapbook paper and glue on each side of the ornament with decoupage medium. Let dry. Coat the paper surfaces with two coats of decoupage medium. Let dry.
4. Glue a flattened bottle cap to the front of the ornament with metal glue. (You can place it in the middle or offset the cap to over hang the edge.)
5. Glue the round sticker inside the bottle cap with white craft glue. Let dry. TIP: To make sure the stickers do not curl up as they dry, press them down while they are drying.
6. Apply a generous amount of clear dimensional paint inside the bottle cap to give the image a shiny, domed appearance.
7. With metal glue, attach rhinestones, charms, or other metal embellishments.
8. Highlight the rims of the metal discs and bottle cap with metallic wax paste.
9. Use metal glue to adhere eyelash fibers around the edge of the ornament between the metal discs. ❑

Make Time Clock

This charming old-fashioned clock uses an old stovepipe cover as the base, but you could also use a metal or wooden plate for this project. I used round stickers with words and children's faces, but you could substitute photographs or other decorative images to personalize your design.

Supplies

- Old stovepipe cover plate, 8-1/2" diameter
- 12 flattened bottle caps
- Round stickers, 1" diameter (for bottle caps)
- Rubber stamp – Clock face *or* paper with printed clock face
- Brown ink pad
- Tan card paper
- Clock mechanism and hands
- Metal glue
- White craft glue
- Decoupage medium
- Steel wool
- Awl
- Hammer

Instructions

1. Lightly rub the stovepipe cover with steel wool to remove any rust.
2. Stamp the clock face on the tan paper. Cut out the image, centering it in a 4-1/2" diameter circle. TIP: It's easier to stamp the image first, then cut out the circle than the other way around.
3. Glue the stamped circle to the center flat area of the cover, using the decoupage medium. Brush with two coats of the decoupage medium to protect the clock face. Let dry.
4. With an awl, punch a hole in the center of the clock face. Install the clock mechanism and hands.
5. Using metal glue, attach the bottle caps around the rim of the clock.
6. Glue the round stickers in each bottle cap, using white craft glue. TIP: To make sure the stickers do not curl up, press them down while they dry. ❏

Door Plate Collection

This project showcases a metal door plate collection, but you could use other metal items such as keys or cabinet pulls or an architectural metal piece. These metal pieces are inexpensive and readily available at salvage yards.

I used six door plates of various sizes and shapes and embellished the collection for added interest with a metal label holder, a cabinet knob, a drawer pull, and keys. New and old embellishments can be used.

Supplies

- Frame, 16" x 20"
- Foam core board, 16" x 20", 1/2" thick
- Cotton fabrics (Choose colors to match your decor.)
- Trims (Choose a variety of colors and widths to match fabric.)
- Doorknob plates
- Metal embellishments
- Brass wood screws, 5/8" long
- Upholstery tacks
- Steel wool or fine abrasive pads
- Metal paint – Antique white
- 300 grit sandpaper
- Spray adhesive
- Fabric glue
- Scissors

Instructions

1. Prepare the metal doorplates and embellishments by removing any rust or paint with steel wool.
2. Paint the pieces, using a dense foam sponge to apply a thin coat of paint. Where needed, add a second coat. Let dry completely.
3. Sand the pieces to distress and reveal the details.
4. Plan the arrangement, dividing the board into sections. Position the doorplates and embellishments to create a design that pleases you.
5. Cut the fabric, making the panel pieces s 3/4" larger on all sides than the size of the section.
6. Iron the fabric and turn the raw edges under 1/2".
7. Coat the foam board with spray adhesive. Let dry a few minutes, then arrange the fabric on the board. TIP: Letting the spray adhesive dry means it will not seep through the fabric; it also makes repositioning the fabric panels possible.
8. Glue trim where the sections intersect, using fabric glue. Add tacks at the ends of the trims or in rows to accent the panels.
9. With an awl, make small holes to mark where to place the screws to attach the plates.
10. Position the plates. Add a drop of fabric glue to each hole before installing the screws to attach the plate firmly to the fabric-covered foam board.
11. Position and secure the smaller embellishments, using fabric glue to adhere them. Let dry.
12. Place the foam board into the frame and secure. ❏

Metric Conversion Chart

Inches to Millimeters and Centimeters

Inches	MM	CM	Inches	MM	CM
1/8	3	.3	2	51	5.1
1/4	6	.6	3	76	7.6
3/8	10	1.0	4	102	10.2
1/2	13	1.3	5	127	12.7
5/8	16	1.6	6	152	15.2
3/4	19	1.9	7	178	17.8
7/8	22	2.2	8	203	20.3
1	25	2.5	9	229	22.9
1-1/4	32	3.2	10	254	25.4
1-1/2	38	3.8	11	279	27.9
1-3/4	44	4.4	12	305	30.5

Yards to Meters

Yards	Meters	Yards	Meters
1/8	.11	3	2.74
1/4	.23	4	3.66
3/8	.34	5	4.57
1/2	.46	6	5.49
5/8	.57	7	6.40
3/4	.69	8	7.32
7/8	.80	9	8.23
1	.91	10	9.14
2	1.83		

Index

Continued on page 128

Index Continued